MAKING THE GOOD NEWS GOOD AGAIN

Smyth & Helwys Publishing, Inc.
6316 Peake Road
Macon, Georgia 31210-3960
1-800-747-3016
©2009 by Smyth & Helwys Publishing
All rights reserved.

Library of Congress Cataloging-in-Publication Data

Edwards, Judson.
Making the good news good again : recovering the wonder of the Gospel / by Judson Edwards.
p. cm.
Includes bibliographical references and index.
ISBN 978-1-57312-529-1
1. Church renewal. 2. Wonder.
3. Jesus Christ. 4. Christianity.
I. Title.
BV600.E28 2009 269—dc22
2009002332

MAKING THE
GOOD NEWS
GOOD AGAIN

Recovering the Wonder of the Gospel

Judson Edwards

Praise for
Making the Good News Good Again

I have read every book that my friend Jud Edwards has written. His life and ministry have always been about recovering the wonder of the Gospel. His consistent honesty and keen insights in *Making the Good News Good Again* will fill your soul like a good plate of BBQ in the pit of a hungry stomach. Isn't it time you had a heapin' plate of Good News?

—Tim S. Willis
Retired College Minister, Intentional Interim Pastor
and BBQ Connoisseur

I like Judson Edward's new book, *Making the Good News Good Again*. It's vintage Edwards but it shows that the vintage is improving with time. I not only warmed to his thesis and profited from his elaboration of it, but I really enjoyed getting to know him better, which the book certainly makes possible. As a "reflective Christian" (I like his definition), I respond to the way he organizes doubts, failings and other negatives about the faith in such a way as to recognize them and defang them, rather than constantly being bushwhacked by them. Judson's stories of his family help the reader realize why he is one of those who can bless others. He was certainly blessed. While it's obvious much of what he says has emerged from his preaching as well as his own story, not all can arrange such hard-won insights into a pattern that makes sense and shows a healthy spirituality that can guide others on their journeys. From his life and his pulpit, the gospel is obviously and progressively *Good News*.

—Jesse C. Fletcher
President Emeritus
Hardin Simmons University

In *Making the Good News Good Again*, Jud Edwards strained at a book of laws and coughed up a prize: the end of religion and the beginning of freedom in grace! It sounds great but scary, too. Like Jesus' stories, Edwards books are easy to read, but harder to embrace. For Edwards, religion means laws but we like laws. Laws give us a way to keep score and feel good about ourselves, superior to others. Edwards argues that's the problem. Until laws are replaced by freedom in grace there is no joy in Mudville, no wonder in your church.

—Robert Flynn
Author of *Slouching Toward Zion*

We never know if the older son returns to the party his father has given for the safe return of his prodigal brother in Luke 15. After years of church leadership it is easier identifying with the dutiful son in the field than with the younger son basking in the grace of his dad. Judson Edwards reminds us of God's invitation to join the party in his book, *Making the Good News Good Again*. His book is a refreshing summons to experience and reflect the grace of Christ with a world created to know God.

—Randel Everett
Executive Director
Baptist General Convention of Texas

Making Good News Good Again is a conversation about revival, initiated by a careful and compassionate observer of the Christian spirit. Edwards' honesty about the trials and travails of trying to live the faith—particularly what Christians do to diminish each other—rings true. As I read this book, I couldn't help but think about its timeliness, coming to us when countless Christians are disheartened by church conflict, dispirited by the fatigue of doing good, and discouraged by a faltering economy. Yet Edwards' faithful patience provides new lenses for seeing the Christian life in a broader perspective, as well as for reminding us of the divine interconnection between grace and joy.

—Marv Knox
Editor, *The Baptist Standard*

Also by Judson Edwards

Acts: Living With Passionate Faith
(Annual Bible Study Teaching & Study Guide)

The Leadership Labyrinth:
Negotiating the Paradoxes of Ministry

Hidden Treasures

Dedication

For My Grandsons
Anthony Judson Edwards (5-30-07) and
Bodie Max Martyak (11-27-08)
Talk about good news!

A Word of Thanks

Writing this book has been a joy. I'm going to miss lugging my laptop to Starbucks and Krispy Kreme to work on the book and sip my coffee. I'm afraid I'll have to go back to church now to do "ministerial things."

I am especially indebted to two writers for the ideas in this book and the impulse to write it. Karl Olsson was one of the first writers to tell me that the Christian Way is supposed to be a way of joy, and his book, *Come to the Party*, nudged me to do precisely that—come to the party. Robert Capon has been a constant delight to me, and any time my spirits sag, I open his books for a shot of grace. Capon has a gift for making the good news good.

I am also indebted to the fine people at two churches: the Heritage Park Baptist Church in Webster, Texas, and the Woodland Baptist Church in San Antonio, Texas. It has been my pleasure to serve as pastor of those two churches, and for the past thirty-one years, those are the only two churches I've served. Countless people in those churches know how good the good news is, and their buoyant faith has energized mine.

Sherry Edwards and Jimmy Adair both made suggestions that improved this book, and I am grateful for their input. Keith Gammons and the kind folks at Smyth & Helwys have once again seen fit to put my words into print. I thank them for their faith in me.

Finally, thank you, reader, for taking this journey with me. May we all experience the delight of God, and may we all learn to dance to the music of the gospel.

CONTENTS

INTRODUCTION

The greatest need in the church today is for individual Christians to recover the wonder of the gospel. I don't think I'm exaggerating or "speaking ministerially" when I write that, because without wonder, without an appropriate appreciation of the good news of Jesus Christ, we Christians are "running on empty."

Without wonder, our worship sags into boredom, our ministries deteriorate into obligation, and our witness becomes forced and futile. Without wonder, we go through the motions—gritting our teeth and heading to the church committee meeting, filing into the worship service because it's a lifelong custom, and mumbling our perfunctory prayers at the dinner table. But there's no joy in any of those activities, and anyone watching us closely would not find our faith contagious. Wonder is the fuel that keeps Christians going, and without it, church is drab and faith is heavy.

Robert Capon wrote that we Christians are fighting a war between dullness and astonishment.[1] My sense is that dullness is winning. In the coming pages, I want to give astonishment a fighting chance. I hope to say a few things that make the good news *good* again and help us recapture the wonder of it all.

My notion that wonder is the church's greatest need may or may not be true. I know that we could compile a laundry list of greatest needs—prayer, silence, worship, effective preaching, servant leadership, winsome evangelism, and an array of social issues—and make a compelling case for each. I can't say authoritatively that a recovery of wonder is the church's greatest need, though I believe it to be true.

What I *can* say authoritatively is that a recovery of wonder is the greatest need in my own life. As the pastor of churches for thirty-five years, I'm tired. I can't count the number of sermons I've preached, meetings I've attended, wedding and funerals I've conducted, and pious poses I've struck. I'm on the verge of letting the ecclesiastical hairball overwhelm me.

What I need more than anything right now is a reminder of how good the good news is. I need a refresher course on grace, a tutorial on astonishment. I'm actually writing this book more for myself than for you, but if you're a longtime Christian who is weary and heavy-laden, perhaps our experiences can intersect.

E. B. White wrote, "Why else would you be reading this fragmentary page—you with the book on your lap? You're not out to learn anything certainly. You just want the healing action of some chance corroboration, the soporific of spirit laid against spirit."[2] Chance corroboration? Spirit laid against spirit? If that happens in these pages, we will both be blessed.

Though the subject matter for this book has rattled around in my head for a long time, one recent event nudged me to sit down at the computer and start making it happen. I attended a retreat for pastors. By all measurable standards it was a good retreat. We met at a lovely retreat center nestled in the Texas Hill Country. We had stirring speakers who knew their stuff. Delightful retreaters who were enjoyable to talk to surrounded me. Even the food was good.

But I left the retreat feeling "beat down" and burdened and didn't know why. Something was missing from the retreat (or at least *my* perception of the retreat), and I couldn't quite put my finger on the problem. Why would a good retreat in a gorgeous setting with fine speakers leave me depressed?

As I drove home, I wrestled with that question and finally came up with an answer: when you're running on empty, a map to anywhere doesn't look inviting. That's what the retreat had done. It had given us pastors a map to help us make our churches more responsive to our communities, more sensitive to the poor among us, more aware of ministry opportunities all around us. We were given a biblical "to do" list and challenged to make a difference in the world. Who could criticize that?

But I perceived it as simply more to do, more items to add to my already overloaded ministerial agenda, more freight to cram into my gas-starved car. The information I received at that retreat was a good map, all right, but when your gas tank is empty, a good map is useless.

I went home depressed not because the retreat was bad, but because it failed to meet my deepest need.

More than new strategies for my church, I need new strategies for my own survival. More than creative ways to reach our community, I need a way to make the old news of Jesus alive and fresh in my personal experience. Once I get the astonishment and wonder in place, then I'll be ready to look at ministry ideas. Until then, all attempts to put more on my plate sound like bad news.

If you happen to be in the same place, welcome aboard the good ship Dullness. We have a problem, and we might as well admit it. We desperately need astonishment. We need to splash around in grace a while and come out laughing and feeling frisky again. We need to hear the good news with new ears so that it will become good again.

Frankly, for most of us who have been Christians for a long time, it will not be easy. I once heard someone described as "a good woman, in the worst sense of the word." Most of us, sadly, are "good Christians, in the worst sense of the word." We've been trudging to church activities so long, laboring in the vineyard of the Lord so long, and stuck in a rut so long that we might not be able to dance even if we want to. We've also learned some bad theology along the way, which guarantees we will never learn to dance.

But for our joy's sake, for the sake of those who know us and have to put up with us, and for the sake of the kingdom of God, we need to give it a try. We need to open up, loosen up, laugh a little, and maybe even shed a tear or two at the incredible news that is ours in Jesus Christ. I know that news is good enough to set even the bumbling, hesitant feet of "good Christians" to tapping—if only we can get rid of the religious noise in our heads and hear the sweet, undistilled melody of the gospel.

Jesus said, "Whoever has ears to hear, let that person hear." Here's hoping we "good Christians" do hear—and will hear.

Notes

1. Robert Capon, *The Astonished Heart* (Grand Rapids: Eerdmans, 1996), 120.

2. E. B. White, *One Man's Meat* (New York: Harper & Row, 1944), 79.

Part 1

The Good
News Lost

Chapter 1

WHERE DID THE GOOD NEWS GO?

Forty years ago when my parents moved into their home in Houston, they were thrilled that it had carpet in every room except the kitchen. In those days, having a fully carpeted house was quite a deal. My parents had never had a completely carpeted house before, so they felt like rich folks when they moved into their new place on Candace Street.

They lived in that house for thirty years, and over time those carpets became worn and stained and needed replacing. When my parents died, my brother and his family moved into the house and quickly made a surprising discovery: beneath that old carpet was a solid wood floor with great potential beauty. My brother and his wife hired workers to remove the old carpet. Layer by layer they pulled it out—carpet, dust, molded padding, dead insects, and who knows what else. Removing that old carpet must have been an awful job.

But it was worth it. Sure enough, underneath those layers was a gorgeous wood floor—at least after it had been sanded, polished, and restored to its initial luster. Now, when I go in that house I notice how great those woods floors look. I think how surprised my parents would be to know that the carpet is gone and the wood floors restored.

I tell you this story because I think it speaks to us "good Christians" and what needs to happen in our lives. Unfortunately, we've accumulated a lot of nasty stuff in our spiritual houses. We've added layer after layer of worship services, doctrines, meetings, church politics, weird people, and bizarre preachers. Gradually, over the years, we've accumulated a dusty faith tainted by mold and who knows what else. But somehow we know that underneath all that crud lies something beautiful. If we could just peel away the layers that have built up over the years, we would discover it. We would discover the gospel, the good news of Jesus Christ. We would remember why the Christian message is called the good news—not the bad news, or the obligatory news, or the boring news. Once again, our hearts would be glad, and we would laugh more and sing louder and eat more ice cream.

Getting through all of those layers will not be easy or fun. Like my parents, we're proud of our carpeted spiritual houses—even if they are dirty and making us sick. It's no easy task for anyone to remove old habits and haul off old traditions. Sacred cows do not go softly into the night; they exit screaming and cursing.

But the prize is worth the effort. Wouldn't it be great if the Bible fascinated us once again? Wouldn't we do almost anything to sense the presence of God anew in our lives? Wouldn't we love to return to the truths that matter and stop haggling over trivia? Wouldn't we pay almost anything to get the wonder back?

Of course we would, but those things can't happen unless we realize our plight and start tearing out old carpet. Some significant things—historically and personally—need to go. We might as well roll up our sleeves, slog into the den, and start the process.

Warp Speed through History

At the risk of doing grave injustice to church history, I want to race through the centuries at warp speed to show you some of the layers of religion loaded onto our faith. Every respectable church historian who reads this will no doubt scoff at my treatment of church history, but I'll take that chance simply because I want you to see how much unnecessary baggage most of us carry. I'm not trying to teach you church history, really; I just want you to see how, through the centuries, the good news got obscured by religion and became bad news.

Herewith, a warp-speed look at church history:

A Community of Good News. The first Christians saw themselves as recipients of an amazing story and witnesses of amazing events. They knew Jesus had been crucified. They saw him alive after that crucifixion. Then they experienced wind, fire, tongues, and power at Pentecost. They were not forming a new religion, nor were they establishing a new religious institution. If you had asked those first Christians what brand of religion they practiced, they would have said, "Jewish." If you had asked them what institutions governed their lives, they would have said the temple and the synagogue. They were simply Jewish people who had seen and heard incredible events, and they lived in celebration of what they had seen and heard.

Luke's description of this band of believers in the book of Acts shows how non-religious and non-institutional this group was:

> Awe came upon everyone, because many wonders and signs were being done by the apostles. All who believed were together and had all things in common; they would sell their possessions and goods and distribute the proceeds to all, as any had need. Day by day, they spent much time together in the temple, they broke bread at home and ate their food with glad and generous hearts, praising God and having the goodwill of all the people. And day by day the Lord added to their number those who were being saved. (Acts 2:43-47)

It is obvious that those people enjoyed eating, worshiping, and celebrating together and taking care of everyone. They had no buildings, budgets, or bylaws. Theirs was a community of good news, and their life together was so contagious that others wanted to get in on it too.

An Institution of Religion. The community-of-good-news phase of the church did not last long. By the end of the first century, the church had become both religious and institutional, which is evident even in the New Testament. The Apostle Paul, among others, kept reminding those Christians not to fall away from grace, not to slip into legalism, and not to drown in institutional trivia, but his words fell mostly on deaf ears. A hundred years into its history, the church had become a religious institution.

To say that the church became "religious" is to say that it became enamored with rules and laws, slipping back into the old Judaistic way of thinking. To say that the church became "institutional" is to say that it fell into the pattern of nearly all movements—it got organized, calcified its beliefs, bought property, and hired professional leaders. The joyful community of good news, singing and eating and celebrating, quickly became a prim and proper organization devoted to religious rules and regulations.

The Official Religion. The church rocked along as an institution for several hundred years, and then its status changed dramatically. The Roman emperor Constantine, in his Edict of Toleration, declared Christianity a *legal* religion, and then, seventy years later, Theodosius made it the *official* religion of the Roman Empire. For the first time in history, the whole society was declared to be Christian and the notion of *Christendom* was born.

At first blush, that sounds like a wonderful thing. An entire society becoming Christian sounds like an evangelistic bonanza. Imagine an entire culture embracing the way of Jesus and living by his commands. But Christendom actually had more negatives than positives, and, in particular, two thorny problems quickly surfaced.

For one thing, once everyone is declared to be Christian, no one is Christian. As long as the church was marginalized, the Jesus followers had to make hard, personal choices about following him. Theirs was a narrow way, and not popular at all. But once the Christendom model ruled, the way became broad, and everyone was on it. No one had to make hard choices or face persecution or ridicule. Glad acceptance of the Jesus Way got watered down to everybody's-Christian-whether-they-want-to-be-or-not, and real faith nearly disappeared.

For another thing, once the church connected with the government, it took on the color of the government. The church/state union blurred the responsibilities of each, and both suffered. The church took on the concerns of the government—making laws, gathering taxes, adjudicating disputes, etc.—and promptly lost its role as a prophetic, graceful community. When the church got in bed with the state, bad things happened to both.

Mini-Christendoms. The Christendom model of the church lasted for centuries, however, and it wasn't until the Reformation in Europe in the sixteenth century that a new model of the church surfaced. Once the Reformation took place and various reformed churches were established, the old Christendom model was replaced by the mini-Christendom model.

That meant every person had to be a member of the official church of a particular nation/state. Everyone in Scotland had to be Presbyterian; everyone in Saxony, Lutheran; everyone in Bavaria, Roman Catholic; everyone in Geneva, Calvinist; and everyone in England, Anglican. No longer were people members of one big, catholic church; now they were members of their own country's particular brand of church.

The minuses in the mini-Christendom system are many, but two stand out. First, this system produced religious ignorance. If all you ever know is your own brand of religion, your knowledge is limited indeed. But if you lived in Scotland, all you knew was the Presbyterian brand of religion, and if you lived in Saxony, Lutheranism was your only cup of tea. This system fostered isolationism and the ignorance that accompanies it.

Second, mini-Christendom fostered dogmatism and intolerance. If everyone around you believes exactly like you do, you eventually believe that your way is the only way. The Calvinists in Geneva saw the Catholics in Bavaria (if they saw them at all) as complete heretics. "Our way is the only way" became the credo of every nation.

Instead of one Christendom that everyone belonged to, the European countries were split into religious factions—which seems light years away from the community of good news in Acts 2.

American Mini-Christendoms. Once the immigrants from Europe landed in America, they brought their mini-Christendom model of church with them. There were no official religions declared in the colonies, but, by accident or design, the Massachusetts Bay Colony was predominantly Congregational, the Virginia Colony Anglican, and the Baltimore Colony Catholic. The old mini-Christendom mindset still ruled.

But it didn't last long in America. The notion of freedom and independence made the European model unpopular here, and the mini-Christendoms started to crumble. The new Americans were looking for liberty, so they rebuffed any attempt to get them into a religious straightjacket. Rhode Island and Pennsylvania were the states that initially instituted true religious liberty.

Competing Corporate Religions. Think, for a moment, about what we have uncovered in this warp-speed journey through church history. Robert Capon, in his book *The Astonished Heart*, gives us a nice review of what we have seen so far: "As if it weren't bad enough that the community of the Good News had become first a religion, then a religious institution, then a societal religious institution, then *the* societal religious institution, and then a collection of societal religious institutions, we proceeded to bring forth the anomaly that continues to this day: we turned it into a free-for-all of *competing Christian religions.*"[1]

The mini-Christendom model died in the early nineteenth century and was replaced by the corporate model. Churches eventually morphed into corporations with boards and budgets and CEOs. And corporations, by their nature, compete with one another for business, so the church started doing the same thing. The Baptists started trying to win more customers than the Methodists. The Episcopalians went toe to toe with the Presbyterians. Eventually, the nondenominational community church took on all of the above, promising its constituency the absence of denominational politics and silliness.

Anyone in church leadership today understands it is a competitive market. If your church nursery isn't equipped with the latest and greatest, the young couples will take their business to the Lutheran church down the street that just completed a total nursery upgrade. If your worship service lacks pizzazz, the teenagers will pack up and go to the church that features a live rock band. The people who succeed in church today are the ones who know it is a competitive market and choose to minister on those terms. It seems to many, though, that the competitive corporate model of the church is gasping for air now and might not survive much longer. It will be interesting to see what new model comes along to replace it.

That, assuredly, is a too-quick run through church history. As I said, I'm not a church historian and don't really want to teach you church history. I just want you to see all of the layers of "stuff" that have overlaid our understanding of the gospel. What began as a community of good news quickly became an institution. Then it became the official institution of the Roman Empire. Then it became a bunch of little official institutions in Europe. Then it became a bunch of little religious institutions in America. Then it became competing corporate institutions, vying for business just like other corporations.

Certainly, heroes and heroines of faith fill our history, and much from that history gives us pride and motivation. And, undoubtedly, Christians in every age have remembered the good news of grace and danced through life because of it. But they have had to "go against the flow" to do it.

It is not important that you memorize all of the phases the church has gone through to get us where we are today. It is important, though, for you to see why we have such trouble hearing our message as good news. So many religious trappings have covered it that it is hardly recognizable.

What is important to know, in other words, is that the religious house we have inherited from our ancestors has layer after layer of crud on top of those pristine wooden floors. It will be no easy task to remove them.

A Look in the Mirror

That thumbnail sketch of church history helps us understand what we have inherited from our forebears. In a sense, we Christians all share that history. We have all inherited the same house. What we choose to do with that house is a matter of personal decision. As we try to recover the wonder of the gospel, it is imperative that we know our *collective* history, but it is also imperative that we know our *personal* history. We each must determine how we've personally received the gospel and how we're going to burrow through the layers of religion that have robbed us of our joy.

We share the same collective history, but our personal histories are as unique as snowflakes and fingerprints. We each have a history—and a story to tell that goes with that history. I will briefly tell you my story, not because it is particularly spectacular or entertaining, but because it is so normal and typical. I tell you my history with the fond hope that I can lay my spirit alongside yours and entice you to plumb your own journey with God.

I grew up in the Baptist brand of Christianity. I made my profession of faith in Christ at the age of seven and was baptized at our church, the Westview Baptist Church in Houston. I promptly launched into a life of childhood and youthful piety—reading the Bible and praying every day, attending Sunday School and worship every week (even Sunday night worship), going to Vacation Bible School every summer, being a diligent Royal Ambassador on Wednesday nights, and, as a teenager, even going to church visitation every Tuesday night to invite others to come to our church and experience what I had experienced. It was a life of simple, childlike faith, and I will always be grateful for it.

What followed was not surprising: I went to a Baptist college, married a Baptist girl, took her off to a Baptist seminary, and became a Baptist preacher. For many years now, I have been the pastor of Baptist churches, but, looking back on my personal history, I see that it all began as a child in that church in Houston. Those years shaped me and continue to shape me to this day.

But during those formative years of my faith, I felt a lot of guilt and pressure. The church that birthed me was, I assume, a typical Southern Baptist church. Karl Olsson described our church well in his book, *Come to the Party*:

> The control, the strenuousness, the sobriety, the devotional intensity, the binding regimen of services and meetings have created a profound conviction both inside and outside the church that the evangelical church is not a party at all, but a drill hall where hilarity

is occasional and accidental and where the purpose is to fashion well-disciplined soldiers for the holy war.[2]

Our church was a drill hall, and I became a well-disciplined soldier for the holy war. If there was a party going on somewhere, I failed to hear about it.

Our church had annual revivals when a guest evangelist would blow through our community and scare us into repentance. We packed the pews, celebrated hot dog and pizza nights, invited our friends to come with us to the revival and, at the end of the week, felt a lot closer to God. Looking back on it, we also felt guilty and burdened. Revivals loaded us with heavy "oughts" and "shoulds"—which we all assumed was what the Bible was about anyway.

One of our pastors was enamored with the book of Revelation and spent most Sundays preaching frightening sermons about the end of time. Sunday after Sunday, we heard how terrible it would be for those without Christ and how God would finally exact excruciating vengeance on unbelievers. We were certainly glad we were not unbelievers and that we would escape that horrible fate, but we also felt sorry for our unbelieving friends and neighbors. If there was good news in the book of Revelation, it was that a few of us would escape God's wrath and walk triumphantly into the new Jerusalem. And if there was good news in the Bible, as a whole, it was that we were going to make it to heaven, while most of the world would not.

Looking back on those early days of faith, I realize what a mixed blessing they were. Our church was full of fine, loving people. I learned the stories in the Bible and the teachings of Jesus. I learned, too, the importance of commitment and obedience. Much of who I am and what I believe even now can be traced back to those early days in that Houston church. As I said, I am grateful for much of that training.

However, I also learned that God wasn't happy with me as I was. My faith was a transactional faith, and God's favor depended on how well I performed. Every Sunday I took my offering envelope to our church and checked the appropriate squares on that envelope, declaring how I had performed that week. If I brought my Bible to church,

I got a certain number of points. If I stayed for worship, read my Sunday school lesson, gave an offering, and brought a friend with me, I got more points. The goal was to be a 100 percent Christian, and I tried hard to measure up.

What I learned, in essence, was that Christianity was a *religion*, a set of religious transactions that could coax God into accepting me. If I could simply check all the boxes, I could declare myself a 100 percent Christian, and God would smile on me. The problem with that, of course, is that it is bad news. If the Christian message is that we have to measure up to win God's love, we are all in a heap of trouble—as the Apostle Paul says repeatedly in his letters. The incredible message of the New Testament, I realized much later, is that God loves us and accepts us even if we can't check a single one of those boxes on the offering envelope.

What I didn't learn in my early days was 1 John 4:19: "We love because he first loved us." That verse later transformed my faith, but it took a long time for me to hear it. That one verse has life-changing power, and it eventually changed my life. I didn't have to check all those boxes to make myself "right with God." I didn't have to be a model citizen, attend church every time the doors opened, give great sums of money to ministry causes, preach spellbinding sermons, or do any other religious thing to win God's love. I already had it. I was loved and valued even without my strenuous efforts to be good. God loved me *first*, and my response to that love is supposed to be a life of celebration and gratitude.

Even though I eventually learned that liberating truth and started celebrating the gospel, I kept forgetting. More accurately, I *keep* forgetting. I still have a tendency to fall into that old transactional kind of faith, believing God is pleased with me only when I'm worn out from a life of draining piety. As Paul put it to the Galatians, I keep falling away from grace.

When I think about my own spiritual story and how I keep returning to those "old tapes," I realize that Jesus' story about the sower and the seeds is about me. Typically, I think, when we read that story we move through the hard soil, the shallow soil, and the thorny soil, assigning people to their inferior soil types and then triumphantly moving on to our soil type—the prepared soil that brings forth good fruit. If we're not careful, that story can be occasion for condescension as we look down on the rest of the world and confidently declare ourselves as good soil.

What I have come to see is that the story of the sower and the seeds is *my* story. There are times in my life when I am the hard soil, and the good news of grace can't penetrate my calloused soul. There are times when I am the shallow soil, falling in and out of grace and showing an unstable faith. There are times when I am the thorny soil, beset by problems and forgetting the One who holds me even in trouble. Thankfully, there are times when I am the productive soil, relishing the good news and celebrating God's grace.

I think it is important for me to know that I am all four of those soils, and then to do my best to settle into soil number four and stay there. When I become the hard, shallow, and thorny soils, it is because I have succumbed to particular temptations. I become those inferior soils when I let myself be ensnared in *familiarity*, *old tapes*, and *personal problems*. Those are my particular enemies, and, if I am to recover the wonder of the gospel and live consistently in that wonder, those are the enemies with which I must battle.

Familiarity. I become as hard as that soil by the wayside in Jesus' story when I let familiarity do its dastardly work on my soul. The gospel becomes neither good nor news when familiarity robs me of delight.

I once heard a story about a pastor who was doing a children's sermon in the morning worship service. The pastor wanted to get the kids to participate in the sermon, so he asked them what he was describing. It was small and furry. It had long ears. It hopped from place to place. And it is often associated with Easter. One little boy raised his hand and offered his guess: "It sounds like a rabbit, but it must be Jesus again." That little guy is on his way to a familiarity that stifles wonder.

For many of us who have grown up in the church, this is our most enticing temptation. We know the words to the hymns without even looking at the hymnal. We know all the stories we study in Sunday school and can't imagine learning anything new. And when the preacher stands to preach and announces the text is the prodigal son, we can't even fathom an angle on that story we haven't already heard at some point in our lives. We've been there and done that, Sunday after Sunday, year after year. For us, "it must be Jesus again."

If you have been a Christian most of your life, immersed in Bible study and worship, that is your enemy too. Our very familiarity with the songs and Scriptures and services blunts our wonder and makes our hearts hard. When we stand to sing "Amazing Grace" together, we can barely stifle a yawn.

Old Tapes. My life becomes like the shallow soil in the story when I let those old tapes from my early days start playing in my brain. There's no doubt that those old tapes are still there. Try as I might, I can't escape them. I must work to gain God's approval. I must try harder to be a good Christian. I might be the only Bible some people will ever read. I need to check all the boxes and be a 100 percent Christian. Those messages are imprinted on my brain and soul and can't be erased.

So my faith is shaky. At times, I embrace grace and live in joy and freedom. At other times, I fall from grace and live in guilt and legalism. I have written many glowing words about grace and freedom in previous books, but now I say in the introduction to this one that I'm tired and about to be overwhelmed by the ecclesiastical hairball. Does that sound like a person living the abundant life to you? Does that sound like someone filled with joy?

There is no doubt that my relationship with God is not as secure as it should be. I'm shallow, not deep, and need constant reminders of God's grace and acceptance.

Personal Problems. My life becomes like the thorny soil when I let personal problems discourage me and pull me into depression. In his story, Jesus says those who are like the thorny soil "are the ones who hear the word, but the cares of the world, and the lure of wealth, and the desire for other things come in and choke the word, and it yields nothing" (Mark 4:18-19). Glad acceptance of grace gets lost in a pile of problems and misplaced priorities.

I have just finished an extensive study of the book of Acts, and one of the things that impressed me most was the resiliency of the Apostle Paul. Time after time in Acts, Paul refused to let personal problems choke out the good news in his life. He would be criticized, imprisoned, or stoned and bounce back with even more faith. The more problems he had, the freer he seemed to become. It was edifying just to remember how resilient he was.

But I am not there. My faith pales alongside his. Let attendance at church take a nosedive, and my self-worth nosedives with it. Let someone get upset and leave our church, and I'm downcast for weeks. Let me be beset with health woes or financial worries or relational conflict, and I'll crumble into a heap of embarrassing self-pity. For me, personal problems sit heavy on my spirit and keep me from joy. It's hard to dance when the weight of the world is on my shoulders.

Good News. Familiarity, old tapes, and personal problems plague me and make my faith hard, shallow, and thorny. But, at times, I'm like that good soil. I "hear the word and accept it and bear fruit" (Mark 4:20). During these stretches, I laugh a lot, get more creative, enjoy little blessings, preach more persuasively, and generally exult in the goodness of both God and life. I experience what Jesus called the abundant life and become more contagious in my witness.

My goal, of course, is to live more often in this state of grace. I want to be good soil most of the time. I want the word of gentle grace to get so deep in my soul that I accept it and really bear fruit. I want to cast aside familiarity, turn a deaf ear to old tapes, and not get so discouraged by personal problems. I want to love God, serve God, preach sermons for God, love my family for God, give my money to God—in short, live my whole life for God—because I don't *have* to do any of those things.

I want to love God out of sheer gratitude that God already loves me.

Software of the Soul

Those who know me best will probably be surprised and impressed that I have used the word "software" in a book. I have a well-deserved reputation for being computer illiterate, and they will be shocked that I even know what software is. I've come kicking and screaming into our cyber-world and operate in it on about a second-grade level. I know how to send and receive e-mail, surf the Net, and do basic word processing. Beyond that, I'm clueless.

But even I know this: a computer is only as good as its programming. A computer without any software is useless. When I turn on my computer, a menu greets me and defines what I can do. I can only accomplish what the programming will allow me to accomplish.

I suppose what I'm trying to say in this first chapter is that we all have a software of the soul. We have all been programmed—both historically and personally—and that programming determines how we interpret the Bible, how we do church, how we relate to others, and how we think about God. In short, we all have spiritual software that profoundly shapes our lives.

At least for me, some of the programs on my personal computer are outdated and harmful. They need to be updated lest I live my life shackled by false information and faulty thinking. I need to start peeling away some of the religious stuff handed me by my ancestors. I need to look long and hard in the mirror to understand my personal pilgrimage and to move in a new direction. I need some software that enables me to assess church history and personal history. Mostly, I need soul software that makes me glad, infuses me with grace, and makes me thrilled again to be a follower of Jesus.

I think about software Jesus had programmed into his soul as he began his public ministry. After his baptism, he heard a voice from heaven saying, "This is my Son, the Beloved, with whom I am well-pleased" (Matt 3:17). Don't you know that voice echoed in his mind as he faced trouble, dealt with difficult people, and, finally, endured a cross? Don't you know he was encouraged and empowered by the knowledge that he was the Beloved of God, that God took great delight in him?

Some days, familiarity, old tapes, and personal problems "kick in" and keep me from hearing that voice. Instead, I hear that I am a sinner in the hands of an angry God, that my life is futile and my sermons boring, that I don't measure up, and that a bunch of boxes on the offering envelope remain unchecked.

But there are other days when the new tapes kick in, when the new software is activated. On those days, I am happier, less judgmental, freer, and less worried about the future. I go around singing, "If God is for me, who is against me?" and know for certain that I am the beloved.

My earnest prayer is that I will have more and more of those days.

Notes

1. Robert Capon, *The Astonished Heart* (Grand Rapids: Eerdmans, 1996), 8–9. Much of the material in my synopsis of church history was taken from this book.

2. Karl Olsson, *Come to the Party* (Waco: Word, 1972), 151.

Chapter 2

DEATH BY RELIGION

My children were athletes in high school, and Sherry and I were their number-one fans. We traipsed all over the Houston area, watching volleyball, baseball, basketball, and football games and attending our fair share of track meets as well. Fortunately for them, Stacy and Randel were much better athletes than their father, so they provided us with one thrill after another.

However, I do feel that I did my part in making sure they succeeded in their athletic endeavors. If I wore a certain cap to a game and our team won, I kept wearing that cap to games until we lost. If I carried a lucky penny in my pocket and Randel scored a touchdown in that game, I saved that penny and carried it to the next game. If I was chewing a certain flavor of gum, and Stacy was unusually hot on her three-point shots, I made sure I chewed the same flavor at the next game too.

All of my superstitions were, of course, silly, irrational—and very effective! We won most of our games, Randel scored quite a few touchdowns, and Stacy was one of the best three-point shooters in the Houston area. It was all because I quietly contributed my part from the stands. Unbeknownst to anyone but myself and with no thought of personal credit whatsoever, I made sure our team won and that the Edwards children did well. I shudder to think what would have happened without my cap, my penny, and my gum.

In the truest sense of the word, my silly, irrational superstitious acts were not merely superstitious acts; they were silly, irrational *religious* acts. Capon, in his book *Health, Money, and Love*, defines religion as "the attempt on the part of human beings to establish a right relationship between themselves and something outside themselves—something they think to be of life-shaping importance."[1] My cap-wearing, penny-carrying, gum-chewing escapades were attempts to get the gods to smile on our team and my kids.

Religion is what we do to assure that we win, to make sure God smiles upon us. In other words, religion is composed of all those transactions we do to win God's approval and blessing. But the key to understanding religion is to underscore that little word "we" in those sentences. Religion is what *we* do. It is composed of all of those transactions *we* do. Religion is a human activity, created and maintained by humans with the hope that God will notice our actions and bless us.

Cavorting with the Pharisees

Jesus wasn't interested in beginning a new religion; he was interested in abolishing religion altogether. Capon writes,

> In spite of the fact that the Good News of Jesus Christ (to give Christianity one of its own titles of preference) has been seen as a religion by outsiders and been sold as one by its adherents, it is not a religion at all. Rather it is the announcement of *the end of religion.* On its plain, New Testament face, it proclaims that all the things that religion promised but couldn't deliver have been delivered once and for all by Jesus in his death and resurrection.[2]

When Jesus began his ministry and, in effect, announced the end of religion, the first people to rise up in protest to such notions were, not surprisingly, the most religious people of the day. The Pharisees were incensed at some of the outlandish things Jesus did and said and justifiably saw him as a threat to their way of life. If religion did indeed end, what would they do with their lives? If religion was indeed a failed and futile activity, who would need their services? Feeling threatened, they lashed out at Jesus, and Jesus, in turn, lashed out at them.

It has always been one of the greatest ironies of Jesus' life that he saved his harshest anger for the most religious people of his day. Read Matthew 23 if you dare, and watch the smoke rise from the page as

Jesus fires seven "woes" at the religion of the scribes and Pharisees. Some people get scared when they read those apocalyptic passages about the end times, but Matthew 23 is the passage that sends fear through my bones. Jesus speaks in that passage to people like me—good, moral, churchgoing men—and says not one good thing about them.

A quick glance at those "woes" helps us see why religion is doomed to fail. As I read them, I see four fatal flaws in any religious system.

First, religion is overly concerned about appearances. "They do all their deeds to be seen by others; for they make their phylacteries broad and their fringes long. They love to have the place of honor at banquets and the best seats in the synagogues, and to be greeted with respect in the marketplaces, and to have all people call them rabbi" (Matt 23:5-7).

Since religion is a human endeavor initiated by *us*, it demands that *we* get credit for *our* good deeds. If it's all about us and our religious transactions, of course we want to make sure those transactions get noticed. But Jesus said to pray, fast, and give in secret so that no one sees. If it's not about us—if it's about God and God's acts in history and God's grace—why do *we* need to be noticed? Why do *we* need any credit?

Second, religion is blind to sin. "Woe to you, scribes and Pharisees, hypocrites! For you clean the outside of the cup and of the plate, but inside they are full of greed and self-indulgence. You blind Pharisee! First clean the inside of the cup, so that the outside also may be clean" (Matt 23:25-26).

To be sure, religion focuses on sin. It has checklists of what is, and is not, sin. It keeps long records of grievances. But, in Jesus' thinking, that misses the whole point. Sin is not about those outside actions; it's about the heart. Sin is believing in our hearts that we can make it on our own, that all of our religious transactions matter to God. Sin, ironically, is being religious! It assumes we can make it on our good deeds, without the cross and resurrection. Religion focuses so much on human transactions that it is blind to what God has already done in Christ.

Third, religion emphasizes rules over people. "Woe to you, scribes and Pharisees, hypocrites! For you tithe mint, dill, and cumin, and have neglected the weightier matters of the law: justice and mercy and faith. It is these you ought to have practiced without neglecting the others. You blind guides! You strain out a gnat but swallow a camel!" (Matt 23:23-24)

The Pharisees of Jesus' day pinpointed 613 laws in the Old Testament that had to be obeyed. Then there were interpretations of those laws. And interpretations of the interpretations. Where is the good news, I ask you, in a rulebook? Religion is so preoccupied with legalistic gnats that it can't see the camel of grace. It implores us to tithe mint, dill, and cumin and forgets to mention justice, mercy, and faith.

Fourth, religion places a heavy obligation on people. "They tie up heavy burdens, hard to bear, and lay them on the shoulders of others. . ." (Matt 23:4).

Religion is heavy, nitpicking, life-sapping. It loads people down with laws and commandments. It hands people a long checklist of do's and don'ts. It tells people to believe this doctrine, assume this pose, complete these religious transactions, and they will win! God will honor their devotion and shower them with blessings. But the whole process is burdensome and draining.

Those four flaws doom religion. Jesus saw that clearly and said a loud "no" to that approach to God, but the loud cries of the religionists kept drowning out his "no." Both in his own day and in days and centuries to come, his words were silenced by those claiming that people *do* have to do something to make it with God. As I mentioned in the previous chapter, if you follow church history through time, you will see that it is a journey of forgetfulness. It is the sad saga of Christians falling away from grace and returning to the old religion of the Pharisees.

Every time we read those seven "woes" in Matthew 23, we can remember how adamantly Jesus rejected religion—not just the bad religion of the Pharisees, but all religion. We can use that text to pull us back toward the new, nonreligious system Jesus came to establish.

The Torn Curtain

Matthew, Mark, and Luke tell us about the radical new system Jesus established by saying that when Jesus died on the cross, the curtain in the temple was torn in two (Matt 27:51; Mark 15:38; Luke 23:44). It is easy to read over that line in those Gospels and fail to see its significance. The Gospel writers were packing a lot into that subtle punch, and we shouldn't miss their point.

They refer to the curtain in the temple that protected the holy of holies, the symbolic place where God lived. To call it a curtain is to give the wrong impression; it was actually a wall sixty feet high and thirty feet wide. The curtain in the temple was actually a barricade designed to keep common people away from the holiest place in Jewish religion.

The layout of the temple in Jerusalem says volumes about the religion of Jesus' day. It was a carefully constructed system of works and exclusion, and it shows why Jesus so adamantly opposed it.

As you approached the temple, you came first to the Court of the Gentiles. This was as far as any non-Jew could go. In essence, this was a *social wall* blocking entry to all Gentiles. They could go as far as the Court of the Gentiles, but no further.

Next you came to the Court of the Women. This was a court where the Jewish women could congregate, but there was a wall there too, and beyond that wall the women could not go. In essence, this was a *sexual* wall that said, "No women beyond this point!"

Then you came to the Court of Israel. This was the place for the Jewish men who wanted to worship God, but this was as close as they could get to the holy of holies. Only priests could go beyond this point, and the laymen knew it. This *sacral wall* separated laity from clergy.

Next came the Court of the Priests. This was a gathering place for the priests of Israel, but even the priests faced a wall. Beyond the priestly court was the holy of holies, and only one person, the high priest, on one day, the Day of Atonement, could enter it. Even the priests were "walled out." The *spiritual wall* in the temple prohibited even the ordained from getting close to God.

This was the religious system of Jesus' day. There was a definite pecking order determined by status and rank. A social barrier excluded Gentiles, a sexual barrier excluded women, a sacral barrier excluded laypeople, and a spiritual barrier excluded the priests. The whole system was filled with religious walls.

William Hull, in his book *Beyond the Barriers*, discusses these walls in the temple architecture and concludes,

> These walls were not merely decorative but were determinative of Israel's basic understanding of the nature of religion. They did not serve to simply organize available space in convenient fashion; instead, they literally put each person in his or her proper place in relation both to others and to God. In so doing, they confirmed and reinforced assumptions which were operative wherever the Jewish religion was practiced throughout the world.[3]

When Matthew, Mark, and Luke wrote that on the day of Jesus' death the curtain in the temple was torn in two, they were saying that the whole religious system of the Jews came crashing down. Think of the implications of no barricade in the temple. Instead of saying that one man on one day of the year could enter the presence of God, the Gospel writers were saying that anyone could enter the holy of holies and relate to God. Through the death of Jesus, the walls came tumbling down, and ordinary people could stand before God. It was a breathtaking, even heretical notion in the first century, and even today it seems strange. Anyone can come before God? Sinners with no religious credentials can just waltz in and have access to the holy? We don't have to move through a series of religious steps to get to God? Religious status earns us no divine brownie points?

That torn curtain in the temple is one of the finest images in the Bible, so why do we keep trying to sew the curtain back together? Why can't we just let the death and resurrection of Jesus abolish all religious systems so we can run into the holy of holies and say thank you?

The Divine Checkmate

If you think of life as a chess game, the old system before Jesus was this: If we make the right moves in the game of life, we can win. If we do the proper religious things—keep the commandments, go to church, act moral, love others, give our money to help people, and perform the right religious rituals—we can put God in checkmate, and God will be obligated to give us heaven. We've made all the right moves, and God is duty-bound to reward us. That, in effect, was the Pharisees' system, and it was the very system Jesus came to demolish.

In the new Jesus system, *God* makes all the right moves. In the life, death, and resurrection of Jesus, God has put *us* in the divine checkmate. There are no moves left on the board. As Paul put it to the Corinthians, "All this is from God, who reconciled us to himself through Christ, and has given us the ministry of reconciliation; that is, in Christ, God was reconciling the world to himself, not counting their trespasses against them, and entrusting the message of reconciliation to us" (2 Cor 5:18-19). God has won the game and invites us to come to the victory party and celebrate. We've been forgiven and set free and then given the delightful assignment of announcing this incredible piece of news to anyone who will listen.

The danger in this is that it sounds too good to be true. We don't have to do one religious thing to make it with God? We don't have to give one penny, preach one sermon, take one mission trip, teach one Sunday school class, work in one soup kitchen, or do any other one thing to earn God's love? Surely there are still some moves on the board for us to make. Surely there are religious transactions yet to be completed. But Jesus and the New Testament say no. God has completed the final transaction in the cross and resurrection. Our part is to stand in awe, laugh a lot, and make life a grand celebration of grace.

I've read Matthew 11:28 for years and have always found it to be comforting: "Come to me, all you that are weary and are carrying heavy burdens, and I will give you rest." I've always assumed Jesus was addressing those words to people tired from the hurry and worry of life. "If you're worn out from stress, and sick and tired of being sick and tired, come to me and find rest," I heard him say.

But lately I've read that verse in a different way. I've read it as directed to people like the Pharisees, people who let religion rob them of their "lightness." I'm thinking these days that this verse is directed to tired preachers, burned-out deacons, uptight Sunday school teachers, and angry fundamentalists. I hear Jesus saying to all of us, "Come to me and find another way. Quit struggling and straining. Rest in my grace and forgiveness. You're in the divine checkmate, so relax and enjoy God's victory for a change." In other words, lately I've read Matthew 11:28 as the antidote to religion.

Garrett Keizer, in his book *A Dresser of Sycamore Trees*, tells of the moment he discovered he didn't need religion anymore, the moment he knew he could relax into God:

> For I had called to the Lord in my distress, and the Lord answered by setting me free—rather, by letting me know, in what I now hear as a virtual choir of voices, that I was free; free to watch or sleep; to fast or eat bacon, to stay at the guest house alone or with my wife; free, if I could leaven freedom with faith, to accept my own handi-capping limitations as part of "my way" rather than obstacles in my way; free, finally, to ignore a legion of voices that said I was letting God down if I didn't become a priest, or letting myself down if I taught high school, or letting go too easily if I turned my back on both vocations to write down the story of my turning. This was God's answer. It was not the answer I had been looking for, but that was because God, also, was free.[4]

When we find ourselves burdened by our faith, dreading church obligations, and "going through the motions" with God, we should see a big, red flag waving before our eyes. Our "heaviness" tells us something. It tells us that religion has gotten us in its seductive claws and is sapping the life out of us. It tells us to run to the cross and start singing, "I stand amazed in the presence of Jesus, the Nazarene, and wonder how he could love me, a sinner, condemned, unclean." Sinners. Condemned. Unclean. That's who we are. But God in Jesus has put us in the divine checkmate, and we're home free. It's time to kill the fatted calf and be the people of good news we're supposed to be. It's time to drop religion and hold on for dear life to the gospel.

Choosing to Celebrate

There was a time in my life when I ran three miles every day. I guess you could say I ran *religiously*. Every day I hit the roads and jogged through our neighborhood. I eventually got in such good shape that the runs weren't hard, so I could put my body on automatic pilot and simply enjoy the journey.

I discovered many benefits to those daily three-mile jaunts. I got a time of solitude and escaped "church stuff." I improved my cardiovascular health. I saw my neighbors, waved to them, and smelled the burgers cooking on their grills. I kept my weight under control. And, on my holier days, I spent time in prayer. All in all, I enjoyed my running days and would still run today had my knees not given out on me.

But one day, in the midst of my daily jog, I got a totally unexpected reward: I found seven dollars lying in the middle of the road. It was right there on Pilgrim's Point Drive, on the route I ran every day. A five and two ones right there for the taking. I stopped, picked up the money, looked around to see if anyone was watching, put it in my pocket, and took off running again.

Once I had that money in my possession, I had three choices. First, I could feel guilty. I could beat myself up by assuming that a child on a bicycle or some elderly person walking around the block had probably dropped that money. I could launch a guilt party and feel bad about my newfound treasure.

Second, I could get religious. I could decide that I had found that money because I was running in my green shorts that day and then take a vow to wear those green shorts every day. Or I could determine to run this same route every day. Or I could say I need to run even more miles so I could find even more money. I could assume that I found that money because of something right (and religious) that I had done.

Third, I could celebrate. I could decide to take the money home, tell the family about it, and then take my wife and kids to buy ice cream cones. I could choose to see that money in the street as a delightful serendipity and simply be grateful for it.

It seems to me that each of us has those same three options when it comes to the good news about Jesus Christ. According to the New Testament, God has done something remarkable for us. God sent Jesus into the world to die and rise again to forgive our sins, set us free to live the abundant life, and even face death with a fearless hope. God reconciled us to himself, in Paul's worlds, simply because it is in the loving nature of God to reconcile: "For by grace you have been saved through faith, and this is not your own doing; it is the gift of God— not the result of works, so that no one may boast" (Eph 2:8-9).

We have received this remarkable gift. The question is, what shall we do with it? We can feel guilty about it. We can go through life feeling unworthy of the gift and living without joy because we don't deserve it.

We can decide to get religious about it. We can decide God couldn't possibly be that loving and gracious and that, surely, we have to do something to earn God's favor. We can devise our checklists and set about to perform our religious deeds.

Or we can simply celebrate the incredible gift we've been given. We can live with gratitude, serve with joy, worship with gladness, and be light in a dark world.

Think for a moment about Jesus' story of the prodigal son. When that boy returned home and received his father's welcoming embrace, he had those same three choices.

First, he could have lived in guilt, forever regretting his mistakes in the far country. Remorse, not gratitude, could have been his trademark.

Second, he could have assumed that his father loved him because he had done something right and religious. In other words, he could have lived in a relationship of obligation and good works with his father, hoping to appease the father's justifiable anger.

Third, he could have been amazed by the father's love and astounded by his grace. He could have gone to the party in his honor with neither guilt nor obligation, but filled with surprise and gratitude.

Let's hope he took the third option. More to the point, let's hope we do too. Let's hope we get to the place in our relationship with God where we can move beyond guilt and religion and start to celebrate. Let's get to the place of astonishment and surprise and stay there.

Let's go to the party and enjoy ourselves.

Notes

1. Robert Capon, *Health, Money, and Love* (Grand Rapids: Eerdmans, 1990), 28.

2. Ibid., 31.

3. William Hull, *Beyond the Barriers* (Nashville: Broadman, 1981), 28.

4. Garrett Keizer, *A Dresser of Sycamore Trees* (New York: Viking, 1991), 16.

Chapter 3

IS THE BIBLE
GOOD NEWS OR BAD?

Lurking behind our celebration of the good news is a troublesome fear, and we might as well face it and deal with it. Our fear is that the Bible is not really good news at all, and that our proclamations of it as good news are but the wistful dreams of desperate people. I have already quoted several biblical passages in this book that underscore how good the good news is, but if you have studied the Bible at all, you are also thinking of other not-so-positive passages.

You might be thinking of those Old Testament passages where God commands the slaughter of men, women, children, and infants. Or those passages that regulate, and therefore legitimize, slavery. Or those passages that place women in a subordinate role to men. Or those passages that consign unbelievers to a place of eternal torment. Or any number of other passages that cast God in a negative light. How can we say the Bible is good news when those passages stare us in the face? Are we simply choosing the positive parts of the Bible we like and ignoring the negative parts we don't?

I have wrestled with those questions myself and have come to the conclusion that the Bible *is* good news, in fact the best news ever sounded on planet earth. In this chapter, I'll give you five truths about the Bible that have led me to that conclusion. These five keys to understanding Scripture have helped me, and I hope they help you too. I hope they help you celebrate as never before the good news the Bible declares.

A New Set of Glasses

One of the things the Bible does for us is give us a new set of glasses with which to see the world. It gives us truths we would never know without it and an angle of vision on the world that enables us to live joyful, productive lives. Scripture is a book of indispensable truths without which we would live impoverished lives.

Neurological experts tell us our brains are equipped with a reticular activating system that serves as a filter. If all the stimuli in our environment reached our brains, we would go into sensory overload and "flip a breaker." Thus, much of what we see and hear, for example, never makes it to our conscious thoughts. We can look at a bottle of medicine in the cabinet every morning and never "see" it. Or we can look out at a crowd and never "see" Mary who is sitting there on the second row. How can we be so blind? Because our reticular activating system has decided it is not important to notice the medicine or to see Mary and has filtered them out.

Sadly, God often gets filtered out too. We go about our business— raising our families, doing our jobs, getting our exercise, paying our bills, and so on—and never notice God. But the Bible is a constant reminder to us that God is there, working in history and in our personal lives, and that we shouldn't forget that divine presence. It keeps nudging us to open our eyes and see God.

I think of a passage like Isaiah 60:1 that calls people to see something they wouldn't ordinarily see. That verse says, "Arise, shine; for your light has come and the glory of the Lord has risen upon you." It's a comforting verse but doesn't make much sense in the context in which it was written.

That verse was written to discouraged and cynical people. They and their ancestors had lived in Babylonian captivity for seventy long years and had finally come home to Judah, but home wasn't as they remembered it. Buildings had been torn down, and the temple in Jerusalem had been destroyed. The economy was in shambles, and work was almost impossible to find. It was a depressing, discouraging, dead-end time.

When the prophet wrote the words about the light having come and the glory of the Lord rising upon them, those people probably scoffed. They didn't see any light, and if this was indeed the glory of the Lord, they would just as soon not have it. But the prophet was trying to pry open their reticular activating systems. He wanted them to remember God and to know that if God was in the mix, things were not as hopeless as they seemed.

That's one of the things the Bible does for us. It opens our eyes to see the possibilities if God is present in our world and in our personal lives. It gives us a new way of looking at life. It enables us to see life through God-colored glasses.

Once we get these glasses on and wear them for a while, we begin to approach life from a new direction. Old things pass away, and all things become new. We become so familiar with the biblical story that it becomes "our" story. We are actually shaped by the vision of life we learn in Scripture.

I'm reminded of a short story by Nathaniel Hawthorne titled "The Great Stone Face." It is the story of a young boy who stares so long at a face carved in stone that, by the end of the story, his own face is transformed into the image of the stone face. He looks at it so long that it shapes him in its image. That's what the Bible does for us and why we should stare at it as often as possible.

Think of a few of the key elements in our story:

• We are created by God in God's own image.
• We have rebelled against God and gone our own way.
• God has pursued humanity throughout history.
• We are stewards of the earth and all of creation.
• Jesus came to show us what God is like.
• Jesus died and rose again to give us hope and the promise of eternal life.
• Those who know the good news of Jesus live forgiven, free lives.
• The church is a company of people living and sharing good news.
• God is sovereign over all creation and will defeat evil and reign forever.

Those are some of the fundamental truths we learn when we soak our-selves in the biblical story, and they provide us the compass with which we navigate life. Each of those truths has practical implications for how we live, and our days are profoundly influenced by the bibli-cal glasses we wear.

Human and Divine

As we immerse ourselves in biblical truth, we become aware of a ten-sion that must be maintained if we're going to be good interpreters of Scripture. The tension is between the human and divine dimensions of the Bible. The Bible is both a human book and a divine book, and holding those paradoxical truths in tension is crucial. If we lose either side of the tension, we become less-than-accurate interpreters of Scripture.

The Bible is a human book. It was written by flawed human beings, each with a unique writing style, personality, and perspective. The Bible is not a book dictated by God to robots who wrote down the divine revelation; it is a book written by people in search of God, hun-gering for God, and sometimes experiencing God. As such, it is a field guide for pilgrims, giving us the expert notes of people who have gone before us. Some of their notes are more helpful than others (and some seem completely out of touch with our lives!), but they are indispensa-ble notes for anyone wanting to learn the truth about God.

In her book, *Leaving Church,* Barbara Brown Taylor writes at one point about the convictions she has decided to toss out and the ones she has decided to keep:

> I will keep the Bible, which remains the Word of God for me, but always the Word as heard by generations of human beings as flawed as I. As beautifully as these witnesses write, their divine inspiration can never be separated from their ardent desires; their genuine wish to serve God cannot be divorced from their self-interest. That God should use such blemished creatures to communicate God's reality so well makes the Bible its own kind of miracle, but I hope never to

put the book ahead of the people whom the book calls me to love
and serve.[1]

If we lose this part of the tension and deny the Bible's humanity, we
lose much of its charm. As Barbara Brown Taylor says, part of the miracle of the Bible is that God is able to communicate so well through
such blemished characters. That gives us the hope that God might be
able to use *us* and communicate through *us* also. The humanity of the
Bible makes it accessible and attractive to humans.

Without the human dimension, we lose the right to dialogue with
our spiritual ancestors. We can't tell them why we have interest on our
loans even though Moses wouldn't allow it, why we no longer adhere
to Paul's admonitions about slaves obeying their masters, or why we
no longer believe those Old Testament edicts about God wanting us to
kill our enemies. Because the Bible is a human book and the writers
were reflecting their world and their worldviews, we have the right to
converse with them and even insist that we have received more light.

This part of the tension is crucial. The human dimension of the
Bible makes it relevant, alive, and interesting. We get the privilege of
reading the field notes of flesh-and-blood pilgrims who wanted to
serve God in their own time and place. Those notes are helpful to us
precisely because people like us—flawed, fallible human beings—produced them.

The second part of the tension is crucial too: *the Bible is a divine book.*
It is more than just the musings of ordinary people. God has worked
through those people to say a divine word to humanity. Even through
the process of deciding which books made it into the canon—it took
about five centuries for the Old Testament and about three centuries
for the New Testament—God's Spirit was guiding and leading. When
we read the Bible, we are reading a divine word that gives us all of
those fundamental truths that shape our view of the world.

The Bible's guidance to us is a symphony, not a single lyric.
Through voices as dissimilar as Moses, David, Jeremiah, and Paul,
God speaks a word to us. The fact that they are dissimilar and speak
with different voices makes their testimony even more credible. The

fact that the Bible is a human book makes it credible. The fact that it is a divine book makes it incredible.

If we lose this part of the tension and forget the divine part of the equation, the Bible loses its punch. Why believe a book that is nothing more than the thoughts of sinful people in an ancient culture? Why build your life on the misguided notions of people in another time and place? The reason the Bible can command sway over our lives, the reason we can trust the glasses it hands us to wear, is because God is involved in it. It is a human book made powerful and life-changing because God inspired its authors.

You Have Heard It Said of Old . . .

The third truth I claim about the Bible is that it is a dynamic book that moves and develops as you read it. The Bible is anything but stagnant; its ideas grow and change through the centuries, and the wise interpreter of Scripture knows that.

Nowhere is this more evident than in the Sermon on the Mount, where Jesus sketches the new approach to God and life he came to model. As he sketches this new approach, he does a radical thing: he updates some of the Old Testament commandments. Six times in Matthew 5, Jesus states the old law and then updates it. He uses the formula, "You have heard it said of old, but I say to you . . . ." Those old laws were not set in stone after all; by the time of Jesus, they were inadequate and needed updating.

The six issues Jesus updated were murder (upgraded to the anger beneath it); adultery (upgraded to the lust that produces it); certificates of divorce (upgraded to the act of divorce that engendered the certificate), oaths (upgraded to speaking the truth at all times), revenge (upgraded to grace and turning the other cheek), and hating enemies (upgraded to loving all people all the time). Jesus took the Old Testament commands and brought them up to date. In the first four upgrades, he transcended the letter of the laws and captured the spirit beneath them. In the last two upgrades, he changed the laws altogether.

The point I want you to see is that Jesus viewed Scripture as a living thing, as something alive and sharper than a two-edged sword. He felt the freedom to let the Spirit guide him, and he had the audacity to change some of those old commands. No wonder the religious leaders of the day couldn't tolerate Jesus! They must have seen him as both haughty and heretical. Imagine changing the law of God! Imagine saying some of the Old Testament commandments weren't adequate! The nerve of that man!

This "You have heard it said of old, but I say to you . . ." pattern of Jesus reminds us, though, that Scripture moves and changes. Just because some Old Testament passages say to kill people doesn't mean we should take up arms and slay our enemies in the name of the Lord. By the time we get to Jesus and the New Testament, those old edicts are overturned and upgraded. Just because the old Levitical laws tell us what to eat and how to dress doesn't mean we need to pay them heed. By the time of the New Testament, the early Christians knew that the way of Jesus had supplanted the Levitical laws.

That is why it is always dangerous to pull any passage out of context and say it must be believed because it is in the Bible. If we desired, we could use the Bible to rationalize war, slavery, racism, polygamy, the denigration of women, and the stoning of disobedient children. In fact, people *have* used the Bible to rationalize those things, but the passages that prescribe those practices are not the final word from God on the subject. Scriptural thought *moves*, and wise interpreters of Scripture move too.

The Burden of Interpretation

It makes us nervous, though, to think that the burden of sound biblical interpretation falls on our shoulders. It's more comforting to envision an inerrant God writing an inerrant book that we can simply believe and live by. "God said it, I believe it, that settles it" offers a certain amount of comfort. When we start saying the Bible is a human and divine book that is dynamic and progressive, we have to do a good job of interpreting it. *We* are responsible for making good sense of the Bible.

In his book *Mere Morality*, Lewis Smedes includes a long footnote about biblical interpretation that I have found helpful for years.[2] He likens biblical interpretation to baseball, of all things, and makes intriguing comparisons.

He says both baseball and the Bible have *rules of the game.* These control the essence of the game. Change these rules, and you change the game. In baseball, for example, if you say a batter is out after *two* strikes instead of three, you fundamentally change the nature of the game. If a caught fly ball is no longer considered an out, you tamper with a rule of the game.

The Bible has its rules of the game too. The Ten Commandments are rules of the game. So are Psalm 23 and 1 Corinthians 13. Take away salvation through the cross of Jesus, and the rules of the New Testament are altered beyond recognition. These are the parts of the Bible that define our faith and give us the essence of who we are as Christians.

Then there are *rules of strategy.* In baseball, most managers might choose to walk a batter intentionally if a weak-hitting pitcher is on deck, or move the outfield back to the warning track if a slugger comes to the plate. These moves in no way affect the rules of the game. They are rules of strategy designed to help a team win.

There are rules of strategy in Scripture too. Moses' rule against charging interest on loans was a strategy for helping poor people keep their farms. Paul's rule for slaves to obey their masters might have been a rule for letting the Christian message move out into the world without a lot of opposition from slaveowners. Good strategies? Yes. Fundamental, bedrock beliefs for all time? No.

Then there are *rules of propriety.* It is deemed unseemly in baseball to throw at a batter's head or to steal the catcher's signals from second base or to throw dirt at an umpire. Those are not rules of the game or even rules of strategy. They are rules of propriety that many baseball players believe protect the integrity of their game.

In Scripture there are rules of propriety too. Paul's assertion that women should wear veils when they prayed in public places is one of them. In the first-century world, not wearing a veil amounted to flaunting the female face in a culture offended by it. Thus, Paul wrote, to influence people for Christ, ladies shouldn't flaunt their faces. Many of Paul's other commands to churches seem to fit this category too.

I have found Smedes' distinctions helpful because they remind me that not everything in the Bible carries equal weight. The laws in Leviticus pale beside the Sermon on the Mount. The commands to kill enemies in the Old Testament are wiped out by 1 Corinthians 13. The verses that describe women as second-rate people are drowned out by other verses declaring that God loves everyone and that, with God, there is "no longer male and female, for you are all one in Christ Jesus" (Gal 3:28).

It makes us nervous to think we have to decide what is a rule of the game, what is a rule of strategy, and what is a rule of propriety. It also makes us squirm to think some parts of the Bible are not as important as others. But it's true, so let's make a vow to be capable, qualified biblical interpreters.

The Governing Word

I've been circling around for a long time, trying to get to this point, and now it's time to come in for a landing. I started this chapter by posing the question, "Is the Bible good news or bad?" I said we have an unspoken fear that maybe the Bible is not good news because we know vitriolic passages that make our hair curl. I have sketched four hermeneutical principles that I hope have set the stage for this final one:

(1) The Bible gives us new glasses with which to see the world.
(2) The Bible is both a human and divine book.
(3) The Bible is a progressive document that changes and develops over time.
(4) The Bible must be interpreted correctly, and there is a burden on us, the interpreters, to do a good job.

With those hermeneutical linchpins firmly (shakily?) in place, we can then decide what the Bible is primarily trying to tell us. What exactly is the fundamental message of Scripture, the essential point of it all? In other words, what is the *governing* word in the Bible?

Fortunately, the Bible itself helps us answer those questions. The final, ultimate word in Scripture is not a written word at all but the Living Word, Jesus of Nazareth. Listen to two of the biblical witnesses as they speak of this Word and, in the process, help us see the governing word of the Bible.

Here's the way the book of Hebrews begins:

> Long ago God spoke to our ancestors in many and various ways by the prophets, but in these last days he has spoken to us by a Son, whom he appointed heir of all things, through whom he also created the worlds. He is the reflection of God's glory and the exact imprint of God's very being, and he sustains all things by his powerful word. When he had made purification for sins, he sat down at the right hand of the Majesty on high, having become as much superior to angels as the name he has inherited is more excellent than theirs. (Heb 1:1-4)

Listen now to Paul in his letter to the Colossians:

> He (Jesus) is the image of the invisible God, the firstborn of all creation; for in him all things in heaven and on earth were created, things visible and invisible, whether thrones or dominions or rulers or powers—all things have been created through him and for him. He himself is before all things, and in him all things hold together. He is the head of the body, the church; he is the beginning, the firstborn from the dead, so that he might come to have first place in everything. For in him all the fullness of God was pleased to dwell, and through him God was pleased to reconcile to himself all things, whether on earth or in heaven, by making peace through the blood of his cross. (Col 1:15-20)

The governing word in the Bible is Jesus, the Living Word, who has "made purification for sins" and through whom "God was pleased to reconcile to himself all things, whether on earth or in heaven, by making peace through the blood of his cross." All the strange Old

Testament laws, all the angry prophetic utterances, all the passages that make God seem mean and punitive are finally swallowed up by the governing word in Scripture: Jesus is the full revelation of God, and his death on our behalf has put us right with God.

By the time you get to the end of the Bible, the one overriding truth that stands out is the arrival of Jesus in history and his death and resurrection to reconcile all things to God. He is why I say the Bible is the best news ever sounded on planet earth. Jesus not only modeled a new way of living, but he died on the cross to make us right with God. Now we're free and forgiven. Now we can read all of those "negative passages" in the Bible and know they're not the final word in the story. The final, governing word is Jesus and his reconciling death on the cross.

Here, then, is the final hermeneutical principle in our mini-lesson on biblical interpretation and the best news I can think to tell you about the Bible: Anything in the Bible that contradicts Jesus is not the final word. Everything in Scripture must be measured by him—who he was, what he said, and what he did. When that principle is upheld, there is plenty of reason to celebrate, and the Bible is seen as good news indeed.

Let me offer you one final illustration, and I'll bring my hermeneutical primer to a close. Think of the Bible as a circus, which, if you think about it, is an apt description of it. The Bible is full of color, action, and larger-than-life characters, much like the typical circus. Like the circus, the Bible has sideshows and a center ring. Circus sideshows might include the world's largest man, the world's strongest woman, and other fascinating people and creatures. Scriptural sideshows include the Old Testament stories and laws, which are fascinating and entertaining and make for an interesting read. They also include some of Paul's counsel to specific churches and some of John's wild dreams in the book of Revelation.

But the center ring attraction of the Bible is Jesus. We pass by those sideshows to make it to the main attraction of the biblical circus: Jesus dying on a cross and then rising from the dead to defeat death. Now that is a main attraction worth seeing! Everything else in the Bible leads us to that center ring, where we get to stand in awe at what

God has done for us in Christ. Once we get to that center ring, we understand why the message about Jesus is called good news. Once we get there, we can only be amazed at this miracle that has saved us and set us free.

Once we get to the center ring and see the cross, we know that nothing in the Bible can drown the good news. No matter how bad and bleak some parts of the Bible sound, they simply cannot silence the joyous laughter that comes from the crucified and risen Christ.

Notes

1. Barbara Brown Taylor, *Leaving Church* (New York: HarperCollins, 2006), 216.
2. Lewis Smedes, *Mere Morality* (Grand Rapids: Eerdmans, 1983), 247–48.

Chapter 4

FRIENDLY FIRE

If, by chance, you wake up one morning feeling *too* happy, *too* close to God, and *too* exuberant, I have a foolproof strategy that will enable you to return to your usual, somber self. All you have to do is turn on the television, tune to the Christian station, and watch for a while. Chances are, what you will see will be shallow, manipulative, gaudy, and embarrassing. By the time you turn off the television, you will be duly depressed and pondering a troublesome question: *This* is what the Christian gospel has produced?

When I reflect on my spiritual journey, I realize a startling, ironic fact: Christians have done more to dissuade me from faith than non-Christians. Pornographers, drug pushers, secular humanists, and militant atheists have done little or nothing to douse my commitment to Christ. In fact, their presence in the world has probably nudged me into firmer conviction.

But I have attended scores of Christian meetings where my fervor took a nosedive, watched dozens of Christian programs that pushed me toward agnosticism, and stood in the presence of quite a few believers who diminished my joy. The saints have wreaked more havoc on my spiritual welfare than the sinners!

In my own experience, it has not been *enemy* fire that has wounded me and stifled the good news. It has been *friendly* fire.

Identifying Friendly Fire

When I try to identify why some Christians siphon my joy and sabotage the good news, I have a hard time doing so without sounding haughty and critical. It is not particularly becoming to throw stones at fellow believers, so, as a general rule, I simply suffer in silence. I go to the services, attend the meetings, hear the sermons, and read the books without uttering one critical word. I hope that as I try to identify friendly fire here, I can do it with a kind spirit.

Six kinds of Christians rain on my parade, and I'm betting they rain on yours too:

(1) *The Overly Certain.* These folks tend to pontificate with great authority. They seem to know how God created the world, how and when Jesus will come again, and precisely what God wants them to do with their lives. They live in a black-and-white world foreign to the gray one in which I reside. God seems to shout to them so that they know beyond a doubt the will of God for their lives—and for mine too!

Daniel Taylor begins his book, *The Myth of Certainty,* with a series of questions that helps readers determine if they are "reflective Christians." Here are a few of those questions:

1. Are you, even after years of being a Christian, ever struck by the unlikelihood of the whole thing? Does one minute it seem perfectly natural and unquestionable that God exists and cares for the world, and the next moment uncommonly naïve?
2. Do you ever think, "Those close to me would be shocked if they knew some of the doubts I have about my faith?" Do you ever scare yourself with your doubts?
3. Have you sometimes felt like walking out of a church service because it seemed contrived and empty?
4. Do you personally find a high degree of paradox in matters of faith, or does it seem primarily reasonable and logical?[1]

There were sixteen questions in all, and, after taking the whole test, I determined I was indeed a "reflective Christian" (which I think sounds

much better than a "doubting Christian" or a "lukewarm Christian"!).
I'm happy to wear that title, but the people who give me problems are
the ones who are *not* reflective. They never struggle. They never doubt.
They're certain—and stuck!—in a dogmatic kind of faith that is heavy
on exclamation points and totally lacking in question marks.

(2) *The Overly Simplistic.* First cousins to the overly certain are the
overly simplistic. These Christians are infatuated by bumper stickers
and slogans. They reduce deep theological truth to catchy truisms
about this car being unmanned in case of rapture or something being
missing in our ch_ _ch. (Why, "U R," of course!) The mystery and
wonder of the biblical message get lost in a sea of clever sayings, and
the world gets the idea that Christians are silly, shallow people.

Real life, though, is messy, gray, and complicated, and honest
people know that. So they assume that the gospel doesn't speak to
them in their messy, gray, complicated life. They assume, if they're
only exposed to overly simplistic Christianity, that it is too shallow
and simple to address their far-from-simple-and-shallow experience.

(3) *The Overly Emotional.* Ingrained in my memory is a worship service I attended years ago at a nondenominational church. Some friends
had invited us to attend the service to hear their favorite gospel singing
group. We went, semi-reluctantly, and were immediately immersed in
a different culture. The lights went down. The music started playing.
The worship leader told us to raise our hands and praise the Lord.
Then he told us to look for someone near us and give that person a
big "hug in the Lord." A large woman started for me, arms out-
stretched . . . and I headed for the door! I wished then that I owned a
button I had seen at another, more subdued meeting—"DON'T
EVEN THINK OF GIVING ME A HUG!" This staid, reserved
Baptist was way over his head in that charismatic service, and, though
I stayed for the entire concert, I felt ill at ease the whole time.

This emotional style of Christianity puts out fleeces, talks inces-
santly of the Spirit, and measures worship by the number of
goosebumps it produces. It has a great interest in miracles, healings,
and the second coming of Jesus. It also delights in the story about

Uncle Billy who received a word from the Lord to buy a certain stock and is now a multimillionaire.

(4) *The Overly Controlling.* These Christians, in their zeal to do good and spread the word of God, go overboard and push too hard. Their concept of power is the right-handed variety—dominating, intimidating, even manipulating. To be in their presence is to be in the presence of coercion. Though they would never put it this baldly, their mantra is "The ends always justify the means."

A writer named Derrick Jensen has written, "As water is to fish, as air is to birds, so coercion is to us. It is where we live. It is what we drink. It is what we breathe. It is transparent. We are so deeply affected that we no longer perceive when we are coercing or being coerced."[2] When that kind of power gets in the church, and in the lives of individual Christians, it creates all kinds of problems. It keeps us from displaying the left-handed power of the cross that is the trademark of Jesus' followers.

All overly controlling Christians would profit by this reminder from Anne Lamott: "Lighthouses don't go running all over an island looking for boats to save; they just stand there shining."[3]

(5) *The Overly Critical.* Back when I used to attend denominational conventions, I always dreaded the time when we, as a group, would pass resolutions. Without fail, our resolutions were critical statements that expressed our corporate disdain for certain groups and activities. We were against anything that even looked suspicious! The next day, the local newspaper would parade in its headlines how we, as Baptists, had passed these resolutions, and anyone reading the paper would assume that those angry, mean-spirited Baptists were at it again.

I know certain things need to be criticized. I know we need to take a stand against evil. But I also know there is a brand of Christianity that gets its energy from being angry. I have been in the presence of this kind of Christianity, and it knows little of the loving spirit of Christ. It focuses on law and moral correctness and neglects grace.

(6) *The Overly Negative.* This entire book is built on the premise that the Christian gospel is *really* good news. I'm always put off when my fellow Christians (and fellow preachers) make it sound like bad news. If you ask these Christians if the gospel is good news, they answer with a resounding "yes." But if you listen to their songs and sermons, you have to wonder. So much of their proclamation is about law, morality, and righteousness that it eventually sounds burdensome and draining.

Always we must ask ourselves, when we evaluate our worship services, if people have heard and experienced the good news. Always we must ask ourselves, when we think about our Sunday school classes, if people have learned how good the good news is. Always we must ask ourselves, when we inventory our lives, if people sense in us a spark of joy and grace that says more than words can convey. Always we Christians must ask ourselves if we are agents of good news to a world desperate for it.

Those six "Christian caricatures" are prevalent in our culture and definitely mute the good news. Sadly, it is possible for a person to have more than one of those characteristics—or even all six! By the time we get through with our viewing of Christian television, or by the time we get out of the worship service, or by the time we finish the best-selling religious book, we find ourselves face to face with one of the great, unanswerable questions of life: How can the Spirit of God lead people down such drastically different paths?

Surviving Friendly Fire

The issue, then, is how to devise a strategy for surviving friendly fire. How can we rub shoulders with Christians of a different stripe and not feel discouraged by them? How can we observe the obvious flaws in people who follow Jesus and not become cynical?

Three questions can help us as we deal with friendly fire, and these three questions offer a strategy for making the good news good even when our fellow believers rain on our parade.

First, can I learn from these Christians? The cynic in me wants to say, "Yes, you can learn not to be like them!" but, actually, there is more to it than that. I've realized that, at least for myself, these people bother me because they have something I don't have. My anger and frustration arise from the fact that they seem to have some elements in their faith that are lacking in mine.

For example, the overly certain rankle me because they have firm convictions, set in stone, and firm biblical beliefs that never waver. For all of the negatives in this kind of faith, it is better than having nothing at all on which to stand. I've wondered at times if these people bother me because my own faith is so uncertain at times that I'm a bit jealous. I long for certainty and can't find it; they've evidently found it in spades, and it irritates me.

The overly simplistic unnerve me because they reduce life to jingles and slogans. They make life so black-and-white and easy to understand that it seems shallow and unreal. But what's wrong, I ask myself, with people simplifying life down to essential truths? Do these people upset me because I've *overcomplicated* life?

The overly emotional cause me grief, perhaps, because they seem to have such joy in their faith that my unemotional, ordered faith pales in comparison. Do these people bother me because they're having more fun than I am?

The overly controlling irritate me because I can't stand to be coerced into anything. I can smell manipulation a mile away and don't want to go anywhere near it. But, I remind myself, these over controlling saints are trying to win people to Jesus, expand the kingdom of God, and minister to others. For all of their flaws and faulty concept of power, are they doing more for the kingdom than I am?

The overly critical can teach me that life calls us to take hard stands occasionally and that some things are worth criticizing. I can easily slip into a laissez-faire, whatever-will-be-will-be approach to life, and these zealous Christians indict me. At least they have a base of convictions from which to throw their stones.

As for the overly negative, I'm not sure what I learn from them. Perhaps I learn that morality and ethics are needed in the church and that I shouldn't dub every call to action as negative and legalistic.

Perhaps I learn that guilt is not always bad. Most of all, perhaps I learn that even longtime believers and "good Christians" can garble the gospel. Of all of the groups that set my teeth on edge, this is the one about whom I have to say, from them I learn not to be like them.

The point is that I can learn something from each group, and each group sinks my spirits for some logical reason. It pays to learn what we can—and then be the person God has called *us* to be.

Second, can I forgive these Christians? It is my contention in these pages that forgiveness is the heart of the gospel, so why shouldn't I apply it to my brothers and sisters in Christ who, in my opinion, have flaws in their faith? Well, I should. Those overly certain, overly simplistic, overly emotional, overly controlling, overly critical, and overly negative fellow pilgrims have their problems, for sure. So do I. As I indicated earlier, my brand of faith tends to be overly analytical. I tend to be heavy on thought and light on feeling. I'm hoping you'll forgive me my faith flaws, even as I forgive those whose faith I find lacking.

Third, can I transcend these Christians? We can learn from these Christians and we can forgive these Christians, but we can also transcend the faith of these Christians. There is a sense in which it is appropriate to see these flaws and not want them. We don't have to be proud or condescending about it; we simply have to take note of these six faith flaws and remind ourselves that faith, like faces, can have deformities. We can then vow to have a faith as beautiful and mature as we, and the Spirit working within us, can manage.

Jean Piaget once explored the moral development of children by investigating their approach to the game of marbles. He noted that the six-year-olds tended to understand the rules as unchangeable and infallible. The ten-year-olds saw the rules as guidelines but felt the freedom to adjust them, if necessary. The twelve-year-olds saw the rules as flexible and open to discussion, looking for whatever would make the game of marbles more fun.

I'm not stretching too much, I think, to say that Christian adults fall into three groups—ages six, ten, and twelve. The six-year-olds see the Christian Way as fixed and set in stone. These are the "God said it,

I believe it, That settles it" folks. The ten-year-olds are more open to change and can live with the idea that even the Bible moves and develops. The twelve-year-olds know that the Spirit blows where it wills and that all of our thoughts about God are inadequate and incomplete. The six-year-olds want certainty. The ten-year-olds want freedom. The twelve-year-olds want mystery.

That, certainly, is an oversimplification. Some of us are twelve one day and six the next! My point is that faith develops. As James Fowler reminded us years ago, there are stages of faith, and we are to move through those stages as we grow spiritually. If, through hard work and the grace of God, we have become a ten-year-old, let's not be pulled back into the faith of the six-year-old, even if it is the dominant level of faith in our culture. If we have received a bit of light and glimpsed something deeper than four spiritual laws, let's be grateful and keep moving forward.

We must keep in mind that other Christians do not set the sail for *our* journey with God. We are captains of our own spiritual ships. How others navigate their ships is between them and God. I do not have to criticize them, become cynical, or feel smug that I'm more spiritually mature. I merely have to be true to the Spirit who is rummaging around in my own soul.

Kierkegaard once wrote in his journal, "The thing is to understand myself, to see what God wishes *me* to do; the thing is to find a truth which is true *for me*, to find *the idea for which I can live and die*."[4] Though we live in families, work in groups, and belong to churches, it finally comes down to a personal decision. We each have a solitary road to travel.

I have to see what God wishes *me* to do. I have to find a truth that is true *for me*. I have to find *the idea for which I can live and die*. And not let others—followers of Jesus but on very different journeys—deter me.

I Thank My God . . .

An old joke says being in the church is like being on Noah's ark: you couldn't stand the smell inside if it wasn't raining so hard outside.

Many of us smile at that joke and affirm its basic truth. Life in the church is far from perfect and Christian people definitely have their flaws, but, in spite of that, the church is still our haven in the storm. In a world where it is pouring rain, that flawed church filled with those flawed people still blesses us and gives us hope.

I may have given the impression in this chapter that some of my fellow Christians have been a constant source of pain for me, that I have spent my life and ministry discouraged by other followers of Jesus. Nothing could be further from the truth. While some Christians have baffled and discouraged me with their approach to God and life, most of the saints have been encouraging. Some Christians have caused me pain and stifled the good news, but most Christians have given me joy and validated the good news. I stand in debt to a host of people who have taught me the way of Jesus and shown, in word and deed, that his way is full of joy.

I think of my parents who loved me unconditionally and modeled good news for me. I think of people in the churches I have pastored who have loved me, fed me, encouraged me in hard times, and been examples of good news when I was prone to forget it. I think of all of those people who have written the books that have molded and challenged me and realize how impoverished my life would be without them. The list of saints to whom I am indebted is a long one.

It is easy to look beneath me and see those Christians who seem to be spiritually and emotionally "younger" than I am. I look at them, see their flaws, and wonder why God doesn't do something about their obvious deficiencies. But I also know many Christians who are way ahead of me and much "older" than I am. I see their grace, read their insights, hear their laughter, observe their courage in grief, and know I have a long way to go to be where they are. If the people "younger" than I am disturb me, the people "older" than I am delight me.

Paul began his letter to his friends in Philippi by saying, "I thank my God every time I remember you . . ." (Phil 1:3). I have a long list of people about whom I could say the same.

Friendly fire is real. Our fellow Christians can most definitely discourage us. But lest we drown in cynicism and pessimism, let's keep in mind that genuine faith is real too. Some Christians, praise God, are daily reminders that the good news really is good.

Notes

1. Daniel Taylor, *The Myth of Certainty* (Waco: Word, 1986), 14.

2. Derrick Jensen, *A Language Older than Words* (New York: Context, 2000), 244.

3. Anne Lamott, *Bird by Bird* (New York: Doubleday, 1994), 236.

4. Soren Kierkegaard, *The Journals*, in *A Kierkegaard Anthology*, ed. Robert Bretall (Princeton: Princeton Press, 1946), 5.

Chapter 5

GOD IS LEFT-HANDED

The 2008 Olympics in Beijing offered one thrill after another. Michael Phelps and Usain Bolt were the biggest stars, but others captured our attention and hearts, as well. Still, as always, the Olympics were filled with heartache, too. Some of the athletes with the highest hopes experienced unexpected problems and had their gold-medal dreams dashed.

Lolo Jones was one of those. She was the odds-on favorite to win the 100-meter hurdles and had the lead in the finals until she clipped the second-to-last hurdle. That small miscue made her stumble, and she crossed the finish line in seventh place. We can only imagine her disappointment. She was the favorite. She had trained for years to reach that moment. She had the lead until the very end of the race. Then it all evaporated because of one small mistake. A clipped hurdle cost her a gold medal.

As we come to the end of this first section of the book, Lolo comes to my mind. Our quest to make the good news good again has a lot in common with her race. Our journey with God is lined with hurdles, and to make the good news good again we have to jump them all. Clipping even one hurdle can make us stumble into bad news.

As we start the race, we realize we have a historical hurdle to get over. Much in church history has garbled the good news, and, if we are going to celebrate the gospel, we have to overcome some of what we have inherited. On top of that, we have personal issues to address and major theological changes to make. Just getting over those first hurdles of church history and personal history is no small feat.

If we manage to get over them, though, we have to deal with religion. The giant hurdle of religion looms large in our culture, and many of our churches have buried the good news of Jesus in a pile of religious rules and regulations. The Pharisees reign supreme in contemporary churches! Getting over the hurdle of religion will not be easy.

Even if we manage to clear it, we still have the Bible to deal with, and, ironically, the Bible itself can be a major source of bad news for us. How can we read the Bible honestly and still see it as good news? What do we do with those "bad parts" of Scripture? We have to learn to be wise interpreters of the Bible, and many a Christian has stumbled here.

Then we must contend with other believers. Friendly fire is a major obstacle, and, at times, we would like to run and hide and not even associate with these weird people who say they follow Jesus. *This* is what the gospel has produced? Other Christians pose a big hurdle for many of us.

Let's suppose that somehow, some way, we negotiate all four of those hurdles. We've managed to leap history, religion, the Bible, and the church, and are still running with joyful faith the race that is set before us. Looming ahead is one final hurdle that might be the most formidable of all: We have to deal with the mysterious silence and hiddenness of God. We have to decide how to make the good news good again when God seems inexplicably removed from our lives. It is a big hurdle, and we need to ponder it honestly, lest we suffer the fate of Lolo and stumble at the finish line. The best way to start, it seems to me, is by examining the whole issue of God's power.

Redefining Power

If I ask you to name a powerful person, who comes to mind? Chances are, you think of someone with physical power—an acquaintance, perhaps, who exercises daily and can lift a Volkswagen, or a defensive tackle who, like a raging bull, sacks quarterbacks.

Or you might think of someone with financial power—a friend who hit the jackpot in the stock market or a Bill Gates who has more money than he can give away.

Or you might think of someone with political power—a governor who governs with an iron fist or the president meeting with a foreign dignitary.

Whoever you think of when I ask you to name someone powerful, it is probable that this person has physical strength, financial clout, or political prestige. Those are the criteria by which we in our culture define "power."

But what if the task at hand requires something this kind of power can't touch? What if, for example, you want to mend the broken heart of someone who is grieving the death of a child? What if you want to write a poem? What if you want to teach a child to read? Those tasks require a different kind of power that transcends physical, financial, or political clout. Our current definition of power is not sufficient. It doesn't cover a host of tasks that need doing, tasks no kind of "force" can accomplish.

Martin Luther once proposed that we think of power in another way. He suggested that there are actually two kinds of power—right-handed power and left-handed power. Right-handed power is straight-line and hard-nosed and includes the activities of defensive tackles, stock market millionaires, and government leaders. Left-handed power, on the other hand, is not straight-line or hard-nosed at all and includes mending a broken heart, writing a poem, and teaching a child to read. Right-handed power is direct, confrontal, and obvious. Left-handed power is indirect, non-confrontal, and unnoticed. Both kinds of power are legitimate, and the world needs both.

Since we have nearly forgotten about left-handed power in our culture, we fail to see how crucial it is to our lives and our world. We also fail to see that God has a preference for it and that much of our spiritual frustration is precisely at this point. We expect God to exert right-handed power in our lives, while God prefers left-handed power. We want God to be like the defensive tackle, sacking our problems and giving us victory, but God is more like the poet, quietly working behind the scenes to create a poem of grace. H. G. Wells once sarcastically described God as "an ever-absent help in time of trouble," and we know what he meant. What if God is not absent, but hidden? What if God is not powerless, but using a kind of power we don't recognize? Wouldn't that ease some of our frustration?

When we turn to the Bible to gain perspective on God's power, we get mixed signals. Certainly, there are passages where God uses right-handed power. God creates. God commands. God destroys Israel's enemies. God enables people to perform miracles. God *does* things, and we get the idea, especially in the Old Testament, that God is right-handed. In fact, one reason so much of the Bible baffles us is that God seems to behave there much differently than God behaves in our own lives.

However, when we turn to the ultimate revelation of God—the arrival of Jesus into the world—we start to sense left-handed power at work. Edmund Steimle writes of Jesus' life,

> . . . when God comes to us, he does not overwhelm. He plays it cool. Low key. He always appears to be less than he really is, what someone has called the "ironical man." Like a child born in a stable. Like a young man growing up in a family for years unrecognized for what he really is. Like a prisoner refusing to answer the false accusations of a judge. Like a man riding bareback on a donkey, his heels grabbing the belly of the animal to keep from falling off. God, "the ironical man," always seems to be less than he really is.[1]

In his book, *Disappointment with God,* Philip Yancey writes about another event in Jesus' life: his weeping over the city of Jerusalem. Yancey points out that this shows a left-handed kind of power that he calls "divine shyness":

> That wail of grief over Jerusalem has about it a quality almost like shyness. Jesus, who could destroy Jerusalem with a word, who could call down legions of angels to force subjection, instead looks over the city and weeps. God holds back; he hides himself; he weeps. Why? Because he desires what power can never win. He is a king who wants not subservience, but love. Thus, rather than mowing down Jerusalem, Rome, and every other worldly power, he chose the

slow, hard way of Incarnation, love, and death. A conquest from within.[2]

As we read through Scripture, then, there seems to be a decided shift toward left-handed power with the coming of Jesus. In fact, when we think about Jesus, it is apparent that God is *mostly* left-handed.

Everything about Jesus' birth was left-handed—his unlikely parents, the birth itself in a cattle stall, the flight to Egypt to escape Herod. None of that smacked of a king's birth.

His life continued the trend—the kind of people he chose for his disciples, the kind of ministry he had, the counter-cultural truths he taught, the way he was rejected by the powerful, religious people of his day. None of that had the ring of messiahship to it either. It all seems, even now, strange and unlikely. No self-respecting Savior of the world would act that way.

In Jesus' death, we see the left-handed power of God most clearly. Paul later referred to "the power of the cross" in 1 Corinthians, but when the cross happened, it looked like anything but power. It looked like defeat and weakness—and it *was* defeat and weakness if your definition of power includes only the right-handed version. Even in the first century, Paul admitted, the Greeks saw Jesus' death as foolishness, the Jews saw it as a stumbling block, and almost no one saw it as the power of God. You would have to have an unusual concept of power to view crucifixion as an example of anything even resembling power.

But Paul saw it as power, and Christians through the centuries have chimed in to say that they see it as power too. Only when you expand your concept of power to include the left-handed version do you see the cross for what it is: God revealing that straight-line, hard-nosed force will not build a kingdom of love. Only crosses can do that, and only crosses can show God's decided preference for left-handed power.

Think again about Jesus' story of the prodigal son, which is also sometimes called the parable of the waiting father. Frankly, most of us don't want a *waiting* father like the one in that story. We want an *acting* father. We want a father who chases the son into the far country, grabs him by the scruff of the neck, and drags him home. We want a father who *does something*, not one who sits on the front porch yearning for his son to return. The waiting father seems so passive, so helpless, that he holds little intrigue. He's too left-handed to suit our taste.

However, if it is true—as I believe it is—that Jesus gives us the best picture of God we've ever had, then God is definitely left-handed. Jesus' birth, life, and death all testify to a God doing things in unexpected, upside-down ways.

Strength in Weakness

Paul's understanding of the power of the cross, his knowledge that God is left-handed, led him to want to become left-handed too. To that same church in Corinth where he had proposed the notion of "the power of the cross," he later wrote about his own ministry: "I will boast all the more gladly of my weaknesses, so that the power of Christ may dwell in me" (2 Cor 12:9).

You can almost hear people's criticism of Paul in the background of those words: "He can't be a real man of God, or he wouldn't be having such a hard time. Wouldn't God shower a faithful man with blessings? Look how weak he is! He looks pitiful. He never has enough money. He's a laughingstock among respectable people. You call this fool a man of God?"

Paul's answer was that his glaring deficiencies only served to accentuate the power of Christ. It was not that Paul didn't have power; he was simply defining power in a different way. It wasn't that Paul couldn't be an effective leader; he was simply leading from weakness instead of strength.

Paul was acquainted enough with the way of Jesus to know that this is how Jesus operated. Remember Paul's word to the Philippians? "Let this same mind be in you that was in Christ Jesus, who, though he was in the form of God, did not regard equality with God as something to be exploited, but emptied himself, taking the form of a slave, being born in human likeness. And being found in human form, he humbled himself and became obedient to the point of death—even death on a cross" (Phil 2:5-8).

Whenever I read the Gospels, I'm reminded that Jesus' disciples didn't understand that at all. They expected Jesus to be a right-handed messiah who would govern the world from Jerusalem. What they got instead was a left-handed messiah who would build a kingdom of love by *dying* in Jerusalem, and they just couldn't believe it.

James and John asked to sit at his right and left hand when he handed out cabinet assignments. They saw Jesus wiping out the old power structure and putting a new one in its place. They saw it as the same power structure, in other words, except with different people in the seats of power: Jesus, James, and John. They envisioned themselves sitting in that room as the new power brokers.

Jesus responded, in effect, "We're not even going near that room." He said, "You know that among the Gentiles those whom they recognize as their rulers lord it over them, and their great ones are tyrants over them. But it is not so among you; but whoever wishes to become great among you must be your servant, and whoever wishes to be first among you must be slave of all. For the Son of Man came not to be served but to serve, and to give his life a ransom for many" (Mark 10:42-45). He was trying to get them to move from right-handed to left-handed power, but they couldn't make the transition.

You see that struggle all through Jesus' life. The disciples didn't get it. Among other things, they knew that Jesus was hanging out with the wrong people from the beginning, people who couldn't "help" him. The woman at the well, blind Bartimaeus, Mary and Martha, and little children had needs, no doubt, but they didn't have money, power, or status, and they wouldn't get Jesus anywhere. Now, the rich young ruler was another matter. That's the kind of guy Jesus needed on board. Someone with a little class and clout. And Jesus, unbelievably, turned him away. It seems to me that all the way through Jesus' ministry, the disciples were deaf to the notion of left-handed power.

Let's give Paul his due: He got it. He understood left-handed power, and he knew it had ministerial, as well as theological, implications. Paul knew it is better to walk alongside people than to be above them. He knew it is more effective to lead from weakness than from strength. He knew he should glory in his weaknesses because other people are healed in the presence of flawed sinners, not perfect saints.

My guess is that most of us have more in common with James and John than we do with Paul. Paul proposed a strange idea, and it runs counter to the prevailing winds of our society. Everything in our culture has taught us that power is about money, status, respectability, and immunity from problems. If we must boast, we will boast of our strengths and hide our weaknesses.

When you think about it, though, there's awfully good news in this power-in-weakness idea if we can muster the faith to believe it. It means we can quit trying so hard to be successful. It means we can relax and be the fragile, fallible people we truly are. It means failure is not the end of the world. It means God puts treasure in plain old clay pots. It means that when we lead from a stance of left-handed power, we opt out of the world's system and step into God's.

This Is My Story, This Is My Song

I do believe God is left-handed—both because of who Jesus was and what Jesus did, but also because of my own experience with God. I had a wise uncle who told me to be suspicious of any map that didn't match the contours of my own experience, and I have found that to be wise counsel. My own experience has taught me that God has an affinity for left-handed power. At least, that's the way God has come to me.

I have spent a good portion of my life wishing for a right-handed God. In my earlier book, *Hidden Treasures*, I told of an experience at seminary that seems symbolic of most of my spiritual journey:

> When I was in seminary, I sat one day in the recliner in our tiny cracker-box house and invited the Divine Lover to come see me. I was tired of working off of hopes and hunches. I needed proof. If I was going to commit myself to a life of ministry, I needed God to come out in the open and tell me straight out I was on the right path. I promised God that my zeal would eclipse even that of the Apostle Paul's if I could just have my own Damascus Road experience. I sat in that recliner, waiting patiently for the Divine Lover to come. I was hoping for thunder, lightning, and a voice from heaven, but I would have settled for a still, small voice. Nothing happened. At least, nothing like I wanted. I sat there in silence for several

hours, and my Suitor never showed up. Finally, I got up in frustration and resumed life. I decided to stay on the path of ministry, but I knew this Lover wouldn't come at my command. I knew I would have to rely on hints and hunches more than I wanted to.[3]

Hints and hunches? Only a fool would build a life on hints and hunches. Yet that is what I have done. I am no happier with that arrangement now than I was when I wrote those words a few years ago. I still long for a right-handed God who will shout instructions to me and rescue me when things get hard. I still long for the God who spoke to Jesus at his baptism and blinded Saul on the road to Damascus. That's a God who does obvious things and works obvious miracles. That's the God I still long to meet.

For whatever reason, that has not been my experience of God. My God has been left-handed. My God has always whispered, never shouted. My God has been shy and hidden, always making me wonder if I am dealing with God at all, but also making me hunger to experience God even more.

The irony is that, on those hints and hunches, I've been a pastor for thirty-five years. The irony is that I believe in God more strongly now than I did when I sat in that recliner years ago and begged God to come to me. The irony is that I can look back on my life and see traces of God all over my personal history, and I believe as never before that I am in the hands of a good God. The irony is that I have written book after book about God, not because I have figured God out and want to explain him to the world, but because I am so fascinated by the search.

I can heartily agree with these words of Eugene Peterson:

We find ourselves praying in a dark forest—days, weeks, months without a glimmer of light—and then we're out in the clear and the sun is shining. One day we don't have a clue to God or meaning or life, and then we do. We thought he was absent and then realize he's present. Because nothing was said, we thought nothing was done—but it was done silently, hiddenly. That's the way resurrection happens—and it happens a lot.[4]

The irony is that over a lifetime of hints and hunches, I have come to believe with ever-growing conviction that the Christian gospel is incredibly good news, news so good that we need to jump every hurdle before us to make sure we know it and celebrate it. This last hurdle—the silence and hiddenness of God—might be the most daunting of all.

Certainly, much of our understanding of God must stay shrouded in mystery. There are no answers to our baffling questions about evil and suffering, for example. There are no answers to most of our personal "Whys?" But there is a good, loving, left-handed God who is sovereign over history and over our personal lives, a God we can lean into and trust.

For me at least, one question in the Bible underscores just how good the good news is. When all else fails and the mysteries of life threaten to overwhelm us, this one question can save us. I want to turn to that question as I launch the second part of the book.

Notes

1. Edmund Steimle, *From Death to Birth* (Philadelphia: Fortress, 1973), 71.

2. Philip Yancey, *Disappointment with God* (Grand Rapids: Zondervan, 1988), 115.

3. Judson Edwards, *Hidden Treasures* (Macon: Smyth & Helwys, 2007), 60–61.

4. Eugene Peterson, *Leap Over a Wall* (San Francisco: Harper, 1997), 228–29.

Part 2

The Good
News Found

Chapter 6

THE QUESTION THAT MAKES ALL THE DIFFERENCE

When I was in elementary school, I lived in fear of Doyle Jennings. He was a few years older than me, and he lived in the house on the corner by the elementary school. Doyle had a reputation as the neighborhood bully, and rumor had it that he enjoyed pummeling younger kids just for the fun of it. I avoided him at all costs and even was afraid to ride my bicycle by his house.

One day, though, I met Doyle face to face and discovered he wasn't the monster we had made him out to be. He was actually friendly to me, and he and I got along well. After that meeting, I no longer feared him and felt free to ride my bike by his house and even to stop and visit him occasionally. Doyle's reputation, it turned out, was much worse than Doyle.

Like Doyle, God has somehow gotten a bad reputation. Our mouths say God is love, but our hearts say otherwise. Somewhere deep down in our hearts is the fear that God is making a list and checking it twice, trying to find out who's naughty and nice. Since we know we're not particularly nice, that is not good news at all. We plaster "God Loves You" on our bumper stickers but secretly live in dread of a God who will condemn us if we fail to measure up.

If we are ever going to make the good news good again, we need a good God. Our theology is crucial to our lives, and we eventually become shaped in the image of our God. The best place I know to discover a good God is in the eighth chapter of the book of Romans. Tucked away in that chapter is one little question that can make all the difference in our theology and in our lives.

Charles Spurgeon once commented that he would rather live in the eighth chapter of Romans than in the beautiful Garden of Eden, because in Romans 8 he was surrounded by "no condemnation" on one side and "no separation" on the other. He's right. Romans 8 is where we Christians need to live. It begins with the promise that "there is therefore now no condemnation for those who are in Christ Jesus" (Rom 8:1), and it ends by celebrating that nothing in all of creation "will be able to separate us from the love of God in Christ Jesus our Lord" (8:39). Romans 8 is good news from beginning to end, and the linchpin that holds it all together is this question: "If God is for us, who is against us?" (Rom 8:31).

That question not only holds Romans 8 together; it can hold *our lives* together. Think about it: If the God of the universe is on our side, what can possibly defeat us? If the God who flung the stars into space is working on our behalf, why should we tiptoe through life in fear? If the God who sustains the spinning earth is also sustaining our personal lives, shouldn't we trust and relax and be grateful?

Romans 8 is a profound theological statement that spells out clearly how much God is *for* us. If we ever start to doubt God or wonder how God feels about us, we should run as fast as we can to Romans 8 and immerse ourselves in it. Romans 8 is perhaps the clearest statement in Scripture of just how good the good news is.

How much is God is for us? How good is the good news? Why should we Christians live every day in gratitude and celebration? Let Paul delineate the reasons in Romans 8.

Because God Is For Us . . .

We have five truths to celebrate:

No Condemnation (8:1-11). As Spurgeon pointed out, Romans 8 begins with the liberating declaration that there is "now no condemnation for those who are in Christ Jesus" (Rom 8:1). Those who lean into the grace of God as offered in Jesus never have to worry about divine condemnation. They are set free "from the law of sin and death" (8:2) and can now walk "according to the Spirit" (8:4). As we embrace the way of Jesus, accept his unbelievable gifts, and walk in his spirit, we experience an incredible freedom.

That freedom comes not from our own efforts, but from what God has done for us: "For God has done what the law, weakened by the flesh, could not do: by sending his own Son in the likeness of sinful flesh, and to deal with sin, he condemned sin in the flesh" (Rom 8:3). The "No Condemnation" sign that now hangs victoriously over our lives was put there by God. In particular, it was put there when Jesus died on the cross.

We have in our bedroom at home a small, cut-glass cross that changes colors as a spinning light hits it. One moment it is blue, the next moment it is green, and then it transforms into yellow. It is especially enjoyable in the dark to watch the changing colors of that cross.

When I think of Jesus' cross, it has a number of colors and dimensions too. One moment I notice that it takes on the color of left-handed power and reminds me that this is the way God works in the world. Another moment, it takes on the color of sacrificial love and reminds me that love always suffers. Then from another angle it has the color of identification: Jesus identifying with us in our pain and telling us that he has walked the way of the cross before us. Then it speaks to me of victory: God taking the worst possible scenario and transforming it into resurrection and joy. The more I look at Jesus' cross, the more colors I see.

But the color Paul celebrates in Romans 8 is the atoning nature of that cross. In ways we cannot even comprehend, the death of Jesus puts us right with God and sets us free from the law of sin and death. His death put the "No Condemnation" sign over our lives. Now we live as free, uncondemned people in the world. Or we *should* live as free, uncondemned people in the world. Myron Madden reminds us that those who cannot accept Jesus' atonement are destined to repeat it, and he's right. If we can't accept his death on our behalf, we have to resort to religion to atone for ourselves. If we can't accept God's acceptance of us, we have to try to earn it on our own. Paul wants us to know that the atonement has happened. Our part is to stay "in Christ Jesus" and avoid the entanglements of bootstrap religion.

Malcolm Muggeridge, in *Jesus Rediscovered,* wrote,

> I would catch a glimpse of the cross—and suddenly my heart would stand still. In an instinctive, intuitive way I understood that some-thing more important, more tumultuous, more passionate, was at issue than our good causes, however noble they might be. . . . I should have worn it. . . . It should have been my uniform, my lan-guage, my life. I shall have no excuse; I can't say I didn't know. I knew from the beginning, and turned away.[1]

If we can "wear" the cross and make it our uniform, our language, our life, we become free people. We have been atoned for, set free, and rescued from condemnation by a gift we can only receive with grateful awe.

No Fear (8:12-17). I remember well a conversation I had with a woman who came to see me about what she called "a spiritual prob-lem." It turned out that her spiritual problem was her fear of God. She had grown up in the church and had been a Christian most of her life, but the "Doyle Jennings Syndrome" ran rampant in her mind. She thought of God as bad, as a bully intent on doing her harm, and she couldn't move beyond that negative concept. I spoke to her of the good news, of how Jesus was God's way of getting rid of a bad reputa-tion, of how God was *for* us, but I'm not sure I was able to change her thinking. It is not easy to remove theological concepts imbedded in a person's mind since childhood.

Paul wants that fearful woman to know that "you did not receive a spirit of slavery to fall back into fear, but you have received a spirit of adoption. When we cry 'Abba! Father!' it is that very Spirit bearing witness with our spirit that we are children of God" (Rom 8:16). God is our "Abba," our Daddy, who loves us personally and profoundly, and any of us who are parents know the depth of that love.

John reminds us later in the New Testament that "there is no fear in love, but perfect love casts out fear; for fear has to do with punishment, and whoever fears has not reached perfection in love" (1 John 4:18). There will come a day, perhaps, when that woman who came to see me will embrace that truth. And there will come a day, perhaps, when you and I will glimpse just how much Abba loves us, just how much delight God takes in us. When that day comes, all fear of God will disappear.

No Despair (8:18-25). I learned a new word recently. *Derapage* is a French word that literally means "slipping" and describes a condition of degeneration, of something or someone spinning out of control. Social *derapage* refers to a culture losing its way, winding down, sinking into ruin. Spiritual *derapage* refers to a person or culture who has lost spiritual passion, who has drifted into apathy. I suppose this book is actually an attempt to keep us from *derapage*, from falling away from grace.

I thought about that word as I read Romans 8:18-25. In those verses, Paul describes creation's *derapage*, how "creation was subjected to futility," "in bondage to decay," and "groaning in labor pains" yearning for rebirth. The whole creation is in a state of *derapage*, according to Paul, but the one who is "in Christ" is rescued from despair and implanted with hope. All that happens to us in our degenerating world cannot be compared with the glory we will experience in eternity, he says. Even now, this side of eternity, we live with hope, a hope that is not seen but *believed.*

For years, I have begun each day with the newspaper and a cup of coffee (okay, several cups of coffee). Most mornings that routine brings me face to face with creation's *derapage*. I read of murders in our city, war in Iraq, the toll pollution has taken on our streams, the plummeting stock market, and dozens of other tragic situations that corroborate Paul's assessment that the creation is subjected to futility and in bondage to decay. More and more, reading the morning newspaper is an act of courage.

Then I think about my personal problems, the problems in our church, and the problems some of our friends and family face, and I see it again: things seem to be falling apart. *Derapage* is the order of the day.

It is tempting in such a world to lose heart, but I refuse to do it. Because I know God is *for* me, I might tiptoe at times to the edge of despair, but I will never fall in. I will remember the One who loves me and is working in my life, and I will get an injection of hope.

No Lostness (8:26-30). Another great chapter in the Bible is Luke 15 where Jesus tells three stories about things that got lost: a lost sheep, a lost coin, and a lost son. In each of those stories, what is lost gets found and then there is a party. The point of all three stories is the same: God is in "the finding business," and when the lost get found the only appropriate response is celebration.

Paul celebrates that same truth in Romans 8: Those in Christ never have to worry about getting lost. God knows each of us and wants the best for us. In fact, in Christ Jesus, God has already found us, so why not let the party begin now?

Even when we feel lost, we should know that God is working in our lives. On those days when we feel deserted by God and don't know how to pray or even want to pray, "the Spirit intercedes with sighs too deep for words. And God, who searches the heart, knows what is the mind of the Spirit, because the Spirit intercedes for the saints according to the will of God" (Rom 8:27). On those days when we feel lost and lonely, the Spirit still works on our behalf.

When we face situations that seem daunting and destructive, "We know that all things work together for good for those who love God, who are called according to his purpose" (Rom 8:28). Some of the strands in the fabric will, no doubt, be dark, but God is stitching something beautiful in our lives. God is taking all of it—the joys and sorrows, the good times and the bad—and weaving a unique tapestry that bears a divine imprint. We are *held, found,* and never need to doubt the sovereignty of God over our lives. We have been predestined, Paul says, then called, justified, and glorified. God *knows* us and is working to glorify us.

Occasionally, when spiritual *derapage* sets in, we fall back into the notion that God is an absentee landlord, checking on us from time to time, but not active in our daily lives. We don't doubt that God exists; we simply doubt that God is doing anything on our behalf today. Jesus, however, begs to differ: "Are not two sparrows sold for a penny? Yet not one of them will fall to the ground apart from your Father. And even the hairs of your head are all counted. So do not be afraid; you are of more value than many sparrows" (Matt 10:29-31). I ask you now: If God knows the number of hairs on your head, don't you suppose that God also knows about your marriage problems, your prodigal child, your job misery, and your financial troubles? Don't you suppose that Jesus is trying to tell us never to doubt the sovereignty of this Father?

God is *for* us, and the same sovereign God Jesus described in Luke 15 and Paul described in Romans 8 is working in our lives. We will not be forgotten, and we will not get lost.

No Separation (8:31-39). Paul concludes his celebration of the character of God by saying that nothing in all of creation can separate us from God's love as revealed in Jesus. Paul runs the gauntlet of horrible things—hardship, distress, persecution, famine, nakedness, peril, sword—and comes out singing on the other side. None of these horrible things can overcome God's sovereign love. "No, in all these things we are more than conquerors through him who loved us" (Rom 8:37).

These final verses of Romans 8 are beautifully written, and Paul is to be commended for his lyrical, poetic words. But what makes these verses so moving is not just that Paul has written them so well, but that Paul has *lived* them so well. These verses are Paul's testimony. He has experienced every condition he mentions and has found God to be faithfully with him through every one of them.

In 2 Corinthians 11, Paul tells his story to the Corinthian Christians and reminds them how he has suffered for the cause of Christ. He says he has been flogged, beaten with lashes, beaten with rods, and stoned. He has been shipwrecked and adrift at sea. He has known countless dangers and endured many sleepless nights. He has been hungry, thirsty, cold, and naked. In other words, he has experienced every miserable condition he lists in Romans 8. But God has never left him, so his words about no separation are convincing. This is not speculation; this is one man's honest story.

To underscore his point, Paul runs another gauntlet of ominous obstacles—death, life, angels, rulers, things present, thing to come, powers, height, depth, anything else in all of creation—and comes out singing again. Nothing "will be able to separate us from the love of God in Christ Jesus our Lord" (Rom 8:39). The chapter ends with Paul singing those words at the top of his voice and celebrating the steadfast character of a God who has never left him.

These are the five truths Paul celebrates in Romans 8, and they are held together by the question that makes all the difference: "If God is for us, who is against us?" Twenty times in this one chapter, Paul uses the word "Spirit," because all that he celebrates here is God's work, God's doing. It is God's Spirit at work freeing us from condemnation. It is God's Spirit who removes our fear and makes us children of God. It is God's Spirit who gives us hope and keeps us from despair. It is God's Spirit who seeks us and finds us. And it is God's Spirit who assures us that nothing we ever experience can separate us from God's love. It is all God's initiative, and it is all worth celebrating.

In spite of this remarkable question and its remarkable implications, *derapage* does set in from time to time. We forget how good God is, how good the good news is, and we stumble into worry, fear, and bad theology. I know firsthand how easy it is to forget the truths of Romans 8 and fall back into bondage.

Driving the Tractor

I spent part of my recent vacation sitting atop a John Deere tractor mowing a field. For the past three years, we have spent a part of the summer with friends in Oregon, and this past summer, to "earn my keep," I volunteered to mow the field. The place where we stay has sixty acres of land, so some part of it always needs mowing. One morning I got on Chet Rawie's John Deere and pointed it toward a grassy field.

As you probably know, mowing a field is not exactly brain surgery. You sit on a tractor and go around and around the field for hours. Any eight-year-old could do it. It's a mindless task, but it offers an opportunity to think. Out there on the tractor, you can shift your mind into any gear you choose. I had no music or distractions of any kind—just me, my thoughts, and the roar of the tractor.

For some strange reason, I decided to shift my mind into a gear marked "W" for Worry. As I circled the field on the tractor, I started thinking about my many worries. I started worrying about the church and some internal squabbling. Then I started worrying about specific people in the church who were dealing with tough problems and difficult situations. After I worried about the church for a while, I started worrying about our country—specifically the war in Iraq.

Then I got personal with my worries and started worrying about myself. Some day in the not-too-distant future, I will no doubt retire. Will I have enough money? What will I do with myself in retirement? Where will we live? That led me to start worrying about our house. I had heard that there are plans to widen the street right behind our house. Are we going to have a super highway running through our back yard? What will that do to the noise level? If we ever want to sell the house, will it be impossible because of the cars zooming through the master bedroom?

When you're out there driving the tractor, you can think of all kinds of things to worry about. One good worry deserves another until you find yourself in a mini-panic. Then I opened my eyes and looked around and realized what a fool I was. It was about 75 degrees with a nice breeze. I was out in the field by myself, looking at hills, trees, and a blue Oregon sky. Why would I ruin that by filling my mind with worry?

I switched gears. I switched from "W" to "G" for Gratitude, and started thinking about all I have to be grateful for. At times like that, it is helpful to have Bible verses stored away in your memory so you can pull them out and reflect on them. I thought of the passage in the Sermon on the Mount where Jesus talks about the birds of the air and the lilies of the field and how we shouldn't worry. I thought of the passage in Philippians where Paul says, "Do not worry about anything, but in everything by prayer and supplication with thanksgiving let your requests be made known to God. And the peace of God, which surpasses all understanding, will guard your hearts and minds in Christ Jesus" (Phil 4:6-7). I started remembering those verses and singing above the roar of the tractor: "Count your many blessings, name them one by one. Count your many blessings, see what God has done."

I thought about Sherry, Stacy, and Randel and how blessed our family has always been. I thought about Steve and Juanita, who married into our family the previous year, and Anthony and Bodie, our new grandsons, who everyone says look a lot like their granddad. I thought about the privilege of being able to write some things that actually became books. I thought about playing tennis with "the old tennis guys" and how much fun we have. I thought about being able to spend the last thirty-one years in two churches and how good and kind people have been to us. I thought about how fresh the air felt there in that Oregon field, how beautiful the scenery was, and how great it was to be sitting on that tractor. I thought about the homemade chili Sherry was making for dinner that night and her pumpkin pie for dessert.

By the time I got through with my gratitude list, it was time to head for the barn. I had been in the field for six hours and had worked up a good sunburn. I had also been knocked around by the tractor in that bumpy field. But as I made my way to the barn, I felt uplifted, not defeated. I looked back at the freshly mowed field and noticed how neat and manicured it looked. It was obvious to me that whoever had mowed that field knew what he was doing!

Until we go back to Oregon next summer, I doubt I will mow any more fields. But I have no doubt that, now that I'm back here in "the real world," I'll be tempted to shift into "W" and start to worry again. I'll be driving the car to the church, or walking around the block, or lying in bed staring at the ceiling and feel tempted to do exactly what I was doing on that tractor. I'll feel tempted to worry—about the church, the kids, the finances, the coming retirement. I have no shortage of things to worry about.

Still, I'm determined to remember the Sermon on the Mount passage about the birds and the lilies and the Philippians 4 passage about not worrying but resting in the peace of God. Mostly I'm going to remember the question that makes all the difference: "If God is for us, who is against us?" I'm going to let that question reset my focus and restore my spirit.

Wishful Thinking?

How do we know, though, that God is accurately described in Romans 8? How can we know for certain that God is *for* us, working on our behalf, when so often we can't feel or tell it? Is it possible that our dream of a loving God is just wishful thinking? Why do we get the right to pick this positive view of God when so many negative ones, even in the Bible, are available to us?

Here are my answers to those questions: We don't know for certain that God is accurately described in Romans 8. We don't know for certain that God is for us. It is possible that all our talk about a God of love is wishful thinking. But it is our privilege and responsibility, as diligent Bible interpreters, to find a God who is the most loving, gracious, and Jesus-like God we can find in the pages of Scripture. For me at least, Romans 8 fills the bill. If God is accurately described there, I can live my life with no condemnation, no fear, no despair, no lostness, and no separation. If I can swim around in Romans 8 long enough, I might someday get to the point where I have a Pauline kind of faith that is exuberant and feisty even when trouble comes.

It takes faith to believe in the God of Romans 8. We don't get to walk by sight here. We have to walk by faith. But what else is new? As Frederick Buechner reminds us in his book, *Wishful Thinking,*

> Almost nothing that makes any real difference can be proved. I can prove the law of gravity by dropping a shoe out of the window. I can prove that the world is round if I'm clever at that sort of thing—that the radio works, that light travels faster than sound. I cannot prove that life is better than death or love better than hate. I cannot prove the greatness of the great or the beauty of the beautiful. I cannot even prove my own free will; maybe my most heroic act, my truest

love, my deepest thought, are all just subtler versions of what happens when the doctor taps my knee with his little rubber hammer and my foot jumps. Faith can't prove a damned thing. Or a blessed thing either.[2]

All the Bible asks us to do is have faith. We are to have faith that God is as good and gracious as Romans 8 says, and live as if that is true. We are to bet our lives that God is *for* us and then see for ourselves if our experience bears that out. We are to lean into this good God and see if, in reality, this good God holds us, sustains us, and nourishes us.

If, like Paul, we find that God does, then who or what can possibly defeat us?

Notes

1. Quoted in Timothy Keller, *The Reason for God* (New York: Dutton, 2008), 186.
2. Frederick Buechner, *Wishful Thinking* (New York: Harper & Row, 1973), 26.

Chapter 7

THE TWO KINDS OF CHRISTIANS

Once Romans 8:31 becomes more than a memory verse, once it settles into our soul and transforms our lives, we are what Karl Olsson calls "one of the blessed." He writes, "The human family—at least what I know of it—is divided into these two groups: the blessed and the unblessed, the favored and the unfavored, the free and the good, those who have come to the party and those who haven't, those who think they can come, and those who think they can't."[1]

When we know that God is for us, working in our lives to bless us, we become a different person. We become blessed, favored, and free. We know we have been invited to the party, so we come and decide to make merry. Or, at least most days, we come to the party and decide to make merry. As I have mentioned, occasionally *derapage* sets in, and even we blessed ones feel ourselves unblessed. But, most days, we are one of the blessed, and we inherit all of the benefits of the blessing.

Every Sunday in churches across the world, two kinds of Christians gather to worship God. The unblessed gather in an attempt to win God's favor; the blessed gather because they already have it. Timothy Keller in *The Reason for God* writes,

> Two people living their lives on the basis of these two different principles may sit next to each other in the church pews. They both pray, give money generously, and are loyal and faithful to their family and church, trying to live decent lives. However, they do so

out of radically different motivations, in two radically different spiritual identities, and the result is two radically different kinds of lives.[2]

These two different kinds of Christians both go by the name "Christian," and they both endeavor to follow Jesus. But one of them does so with a spirit of obligation, and the other does so with a spirit of celebration. Though they carry the same name, they are as different as night and day.

It may be, though, that the best way to underscore the distinction is to point to some people who embody the differences. I'm thinking of two biblical stories that show us a blessed person and an unblessed person side by side. One of those stories is the parable of the prodigal son. The prodigal turns out to be the blessed one, secure in his father's forgiveness and frolicking at the party thrown in his honor. The elder brother turns out to be the unblessed one—correct, condemning, and unable to go to the party because he's too busy keeping score. That story vividly depicts the difference between the blessed and the unblessed.

Since I've already alluded to that story a couple of times in this book, I think I want to go elsewhere. I want to go back to the Old Testament story of David dancing before the Lord and see the difference between David and his wife, Michal. We read this story in 2 Samuel 6, and it seems to be a classic picture of the blessed and unblessed side by side and seeing God and life in drastically different ways.

Learning to Dance

When Lyndon Johnson was president, the media often pictured him as a country bumpkin. He was frequently depicted as a drawling Texan, unschooled in the ways of sophistication. Frankly, President Johnson did a few things that earned him that reputation. One time he lifted one of his Basset hounds by the ears, and that picture was plastered in newspapers across the country. Another time, a reporter asked the president about a recent surgery, and Johnson lifted his shirt to show his scar. Lyndon Johnson seemed to have missed the class on exactly how a president is supposed to behave.

Evidently, David missed that class too, because in 2 Samuel 6, he makes a fool of himself and behaves in a very unkingly way. He gets out in the street and starts dancing, probably half-naked, in front of everybody. This is not the way royalty is supposed to act.

Nobody knows that better than David's wife, Michal, because she is the daughter of Saul, the previous king. She, of all people, has been schooled in royal behavior and knows how a king is supposed to behave. She sees David dancing down there in the street, and the passage says she despises him in her heart. Alexander Whyte once commented that the deaf always despise those who dance.[3] Michal is definitely not hearing the same music David hears, and she despises him. This dancing-in-the-street fiasco is embarrassing, scandalous, silly, and stupid. He simply ought to know better.

Michal looks at David, her husband, and is incensed. But I look at David, the king, dancing before the ark of the covenant, and I am impressed. I am impressed because I see someone forgetting himself, someone getting caught up in the joy of the moment. I want to say, "Dance on, David, and don't ever go to that class on how a king should act, because your joy is contagious. You are the kind of leader we need."

Irenaeus, one of the early church fathers, said the glory of God is a human fully alive. David, dancing there before God and the world, is fully alive. When Thomas Merton became a Trappist monk, his friends were aghast. Merton had been a gregarious, *avant garde* intellectual in New York and then became a monk in a Kentucky monastery. His friends couldn't imagine how he could make such a drastic change. They wondered what he would become, how the experience would affect him.

After thirteen years, Mark van Doren, Merton's former literature professor, visited Merton and then reported back to the world: "Of course he looked a little older; but as we sat and talked I could see no important difference in him, and once I interrupted a reminiscence of his by laughing, 'Tom, I said, 'you haven't changed at all.' 'Why should I? Here,' he said, 'our duty is to be more ourselves, not less.' It was a searching remark and I stood happily corrected."[4]

What makes David's dance so inviting is that he was just being himself—not a king, not a stuff-shirt potentate, but a human being fully alive, caught up in joy, and gloriously oblivious to public opinion polls. He was like a child on Christmas morning—excited, fidgety, his feet on the move. He just had to dance!

It's hard, really, to understand his excitement. The occasion for his joy was the bringing of the ark of the covenant to Jerusalem. For thirty years, the ark had been in the house of the old priest, Abinidab, in the village of Kiriath-Jearim. But the ark was moved back to Jerusalem, and that move set David's heart aflutter with joy.

The ark of the covenant was a rectangular box made of wood and plated with gold. Its solid gold lid was called the mercy seat. The ark had three items inside it: the tablets of stone that Moses had delivered to the people at Sinai, a jar of manna from the wilderness wanderings, and Aaron's rod that budded. Those three items reminded the people of Israel that God commanded them, provided for them, and saved them.

When that ark entered the city of Jerusalem, David couldn't contain himself. He danced for joy. When we read about it in 2 Samuel 6, it indicts us, doesn't it? We've lost that kind of joy, and it seems puzzling and strange to us. We tend to cast our vote with Michal: "Get your act together, David, and start acting like a king!" In our day, worship and church are usually equated with anything *but* gladness and dancing in the street.

However, that quality—the capacity to dance and be glad—more than any other shows we have God in our lives. What is the most infallible proof of the presence of God within us? Personal goodness? Doctrinal correctness? Sacrificial acts of love? I submit to you that it is our joy. They will know we are Christians because they see us dance, because they see the joy in our lives.

I think the shyest person I have ever known was my own mother. Mom was quiet, private, seldom spoke in a group, and dreaded most social gatherings. She was born and raised in a Methodist household, but when she married my dad she started attending the Baptist church. She didn't join the Baptist church until she was sixty years old, though, because she had to make a public decision followed by a public baptism, and it all seemed too hard, too public for her. It was a courageous act on her part when she became a Baptist and was baptized.

Mom was reserved even with us, her family. But one of my fondest memories is of Mom dancing with her two sisters. On several occasions, those three would throw caution to the wind, kick off their shoes, turn up the music, and do the jitterbug. Then they would laugh, start the music again, and dance some more. Sometimes they danced and laughed until the wee hours of the morning. In those moments, Mom was completely unself-conscious, completely caught up in the fun of it all. When I think about our family, I have many good memories, but that one stands out. I love to remember Mom, as shy and reserved as she was, kicking off her shoes and doing the jitterbug.

Traits of the Unblessed

Take a moment to notice the two characters in 2 Samuel 6. Michal is the prototypical unblessed person. As her feelings toward David are revealed, we see clearly some of the characteristics of people who have never received the blessing.

An Inherited Faith. Michal was the daughter of King Saul, David's predecessor. From what we know of Saul, he never had the kind of relationship with God that David had. Saul's faith seems more forced and obligatory. It is impossible to imagine him dancing with glee before the Lord. It is also impossible to imagine him blessing his children or fostering joy in their home. Saul's faith eventually led him to an insane jealousy of David and, finally, to a mad desire to kill him. Suffice it to say that Saul comes across in the Bible as one of the unblessed.

We shouldn't be surprised that his daughter was one of the unblessed too. Unblessed parents tend to produce unblessed children. Michal's response to David as he danced before the Lord was reminiscent of the way Saul would have behaved in that situation. Like father, like daughter.

Earlier, I mentioned that most of us have personal history to deal with if we're ever going to make the good news good again. If we grew up in an unblessed household where we never received our parents' favor or God's favor, we have a lot of work to do. We all inherited much from our families, and we now reap what they sowed. If, like Michal, our inheritance is not filled with blessing, we shouldn't be surprised if we find ourselves unblessed. But the good news is we don't have to *stay* unblessed.

Correctness. As the daughter of a king, Michal knew how a king was supposed to behave before his constituents. She also knew how a king was supposed to behave before God. David was a failure on both counts. He was supposed to be kingly, for God's sake, not out there dancing half-naked in the streets.

Unblessed people tend to be overly concerned about correctness. Doctrinal and moral correctness are crucial to them, and appearance is everything. Think about it a moment, and you can see why. If you're not sure God is for you, pleased with you, and takes delight in you, the only audience left is the one out there in the world. What *people* think is all-important. That's where the unblessed get their "strokes." It's sad, but true: we have to get approval from someone. If it's not God, the crowd will have to do.

Critical spirit. Michal's attitude toward David was one of criticism and judgment. Maybe that's putting it too kindly. When the passage says "she despised him in her heart" (2 Sam 6:16), those are strong words. Unblessed people tend to be critical of and angry toward those around them.

Of course, she had every right to be critical, I suppose. She was correct in her assessment of things. David *was* making a fool of himself. David *was* acting most unkingly. David *was* an embarrassment to her. She was correct, just as the elder brother was correct in declaring that the prodigal son didn't deserve a party. They were both correct, but a correctness that breeds angry criticism will kill any relationship.

Where is grace? Where is forgiveness? Where is the capacity to laugh at someone else's foibles?

As I mentioned, it is one of the sad realities of life that being unblessed is contagious. Unblessed people don't bless others because they don't know how. They've never experienced it themselves, so how can they give it to others? Many a child, in need of the blessing from a mom or dad, will receive anger and criticism instead.

Blessed people become those who bless. Sadly, unblessed people become those who curse.

Jealousy of the Blessing. It is likely that Michal's real problem with David was jealousy. As she watched him from her window, she must have been filled with a perplexed wonder. *How can he be so happy? Why haven't I ever felt that kind of joy myself?*

Jealousy is definitely what the elder brother felt when the prodigal got a party. He told his father that he had been faithful and obedient all his life, and the father had never thrown a party for him. Why should the unfaithful, disobedient son get one? Jealousy and resentment ooze from that story.

Unblessed people tend to envy those who are blessed. People craving the favor of God are jealous of those who have it.

When we look at that snapshot of Michal in 2 Samuel 6, it is almost impossible to be angry with her. We might feel pity, sympathy, or sadness, but not anger. Here's a young woman who probably grew up without the blessing, a young woman who inherited a joyless concept of God. Here's a young woman concerned about correctness and eager to project the right image and do the appropriate thing. Here's a young woman prone to criticism and condemnation, but who can deny that maybe David deserved to be chastised for his shenanigans? And here's a young woman who, perhaps unconsciously, is jealous of anyone who can be happy and dance before the Lord.

How can we be angry with Michal? We can only wish for her a better concept of herself and a better concept of God. Some of us can readily identify with her frustration.

When I see Michal there at her window, watching her husband kicking up his heels on the street below her and despising him in her heart, I see a good woman in the worst sense of the word. She's not evil; she's just mystified by someone who has received the blessing she has longed for all her life. Michal in 2 Samuel 6 is not a *bad* person; she's an *unblessed* person.

Traits of the Blessed

Next, consider David, who, as you know by now, is our example of one of the blessed. David exemplifies traits common to people who have the blessing of God.

Joy. The overriding emotion in this passage is joy. David is ecstatic that the ark of the covenant has come back to Jerusalem—so ecstatic that he drops his royal persona and plays the fool in front of his constituents. It's a picture of a man so joyful he doesn't care about his image.

To say David was filled with joy is not to say he was on an emotional high all the time. When we read his psalms, we know that is not true. Those psalms show us a David who is angry, confused, penitent, mourning, and, at times, overflowing with gratitude. In short, those psalms show us someone very human, but the amazing thing about David was how he did everything before an audience of One. David lived his life before God, and that gave him a foundation for dealing with whatever life hurled at him. Like Paul, David knew God was *for* him, and that conviction made him one of the blessed.

Eugene Peterson describes David like this:

> We're never more alive than when we are dealing with God. And there's a sense in which we aren't alive at all (in the uniquely human sense of "alive") until we're dealing with God. David deals with God. As an instance of humanity in himself, he isn't much. He has little wisdom to pass on to us on how to live successfully. He was an unfortunate parent and an unfaithful husband. From a purely historical point of view he was a barbaric chieftain with a talent for poetry. But David's importance isn't in his morality or his military

prowess but in his experience of and witness to God. Every event in
his life was a confrontation with God.[5]

When we speak of David being joyful, then, we're saying that David
was *alive*. Everything he did was done before a God who loved him
and was sovereign over his life. If God is with you and for you, who or
what can possibly defeat you? If you know God is with you and for
you, welcome to the company of the blessed. Welcome to the company of the joyful.

Freedom. One of the most attractive aspects of this passage is the freedom David displays. He is free from the public opinion polls, free
from the judgments of his wife, free to dance and play the fool
because, frankly, he doesn't much care what others think of him. He
cares mostly about what God thinks of him.

There is an approach to life—indeed, it is Michal's approach to
life in this passage—that is measured, careful, and calculated. It always
takes the temperature of the crowd to see how things are going, and it
always makes adjustments according to that temperature. Erich
Fromm calls the person who adopts this approach to life "the marketing character" and believes this person is the dominant personality
type in our culture:

> The aim of the marketing character is complete adaptation, so as to
> be desirable under all conditions of the personality market. The
> marketing character personalities do not even *have* egos (as people
> in the nineteenth century did) to hold onto, that belong to them,
> that do not change. For they constantly change their egos, according
> to the principle: "I am as you desire me."[6]

When we read 2 Samuel 6, we find ourselves drawn to David's
freedom. He most definitely was not a marketing character, and that is
a rare thing to behold. I mentioned that Michal had to be concerned
about the crowd's approval because she wasn't sure she had God's
approval. David was just the opposite: he wasn't that concerned about

the crowd's approval because he knew he had God's. Blessed people don't worry much about the crowd.

A Desire to Bless Others. Michal's unblessed life spilled over into criticism and condemnation. David's blessed life spilled over into a desire to bless others. When we read about David dancing before the Lord in Samuel 6, we dare not stop reading after David stops his dancing. There is more to the story:

> They brought in the ark of the LORD, and set it in its place, inside the tent that David had pitched for it; and David offered burnt offerings and offerings of well-being before the LORD. When David had finished offering the burnt offerings and the offerings of well-being, he blessed the people in the name of the LORD of hosts, and distributed food among the people, the whole multitude of Israel, both men and woman, to each a cake of bread, a portion of meat, and a cake of raisins. Then all the people went back to their homes. (2 Sam 6:17-19)

David's joy and freedom overflowed into a desire to bless those around him. It's a delightful picture: David making his own offerings to God and then offering his blessing to the people of Israel. Then every person gets bread, meat, and a cake of raisins, and everyone goes home rejoicing at how good life is and how good God is. It's reminiscent of the end of the prodigal son story, where the blessed son gets a party and everyone makes merry.

Blessed people bless others. It's that simple, and that wonderful. People like David, even though they have their flaws, want to bless others and actually do bless others. Mix joy and freedom with this inner impulse to be a blessing, and you have a wonderful combination that can transform people's lives.

Conflict. Honesty demands that we tell the whole story about the blessed. So far, everything is wonderful and well. David has joy, freedom, and a desire to bless others. It's enough to make us all want to become one of the blessed and live in ecstasy. But here's the rest of the story: blessed people inevitably get criticized and have to deal with conflict.

Michal's anger at David in 2 Samuel 6 is one example of this truth. As the biblical story unfolds, we will see this truth revealed over and over. The people who know and love God, the people who know that God is *for* them, are the ones who get criticized and condemned by the world. When the writer of the book of Hebrews does his recap of the heroes of faith in Hebrews 11, he often mentions the persecution these people endured. Looming over the entire biblical story is the experience of Jesus himself. The freest, most blessed human being who ever walked the face of the earth was nailed to a cross by the religious leaders of his day. If we ever need to be reminded of the fate of the blessed, all we need to do is remember Jesus.

There is something sinister in the human heart that wants the blessed to be brought low. The joyless attack the joyful. The captives mock the free. The unblessed look out the window at the blessed, dancing merrily in the street below them, and despise them in their hearts. Some days, being one of the blessed is a real pain.

As we watch David doing his dance there in the street, though, we mostly envy him, I think. Sure, he has to deal with his wife's tantrum. Sure, some Israelites will join her in condemning his display of unprofessionalism. But mostly we envy David's joy, the way he lives before God and is so alive. We envy his freedom, the fact that he doesn't care much what people think. We envy his desire to bless those around him, his willingness to dispense bread and meat and raisins to everyone in his presence. For all of his eccentricities and flaws, David's "blessedness" *shines*, and it still has the power, after all these centuries, to bless us.

Accepting the Blessing

It is fairly easy to point out the traits of blessed and unblessed Christians. We can look at biblical people and people we know today and detect those traits. What is *not* so easy is knowing how the blessed people got the blessing. I wish I could give you "The Three Steps to

Being Blessed by God," or "The Seven Ways to Feel God's Love." Then we could all follow the program and become one of the blessed.

But the blessing doesn't come to us because we've followed the right program. We don't have to *do* anything to get the blessing. The words that describe our part in the process are not aggressive and proactive at all: Accept. Relax. Trust. Lean. Those are the words that come to my mind, and they are much harder to do than following a program.

> Can we *accept* God's acceptance of us?
> Can we *relax* into the grace of God?
> Can we *trust* that God is for us?
> Can we *lean* into the sovereignty of God?

How we answer those questions determines whether we receive the blessing or not. How we answer them determines whether the good news becomes good again for us personally.

The image of a journey with God as a daring adventure needs to remain ever before us, pulling us into something better and deeper than we've yet experienced. A journey with God is supposed to be a blessing:

> The word Christian means different things to different people. To one person it means a stiff, uptight, inflexible way of life, colorless and unbending. To another it means a risky, surprise-filled venture, lived tiptoe at the edge of expectation. Either of these pictures can be supported with evidence. There are numberless illustrations for either position in congregations all over the world. But if we restrict ourselves to biblical evidence, only the second image can be supported: The image of the person living zestfully, exploring *every* experience—pain and joy, enigma and insight, fulfillment and frustration—as a dimension of human freedom, searching through each for sense and grace. If we get our information from the biblical material, there is no doubt that the Christian life is a dancing, leaping, daring life.[7]

I think of David, dancing before the Lord with unrestrained glee. I think of my mother, kicking off her shoes and doing the jitterbug with her sisters. Then I think of my own approach to God and life. Would anyone describe my faith as dancing, leaping, and daring? Would anyone characterize my life as joyful, free, and blessed? More to the point, I suppose, would *God* describe my faith as dancing, leaping, and daring? Would *God* characterize my life as joyful, free, and blessed?

I now believe one thing without question: if I don't have the blessing, it is not God's fault. God has done everything possible to give me the blessing, to shower me with love. If I don't have and live the blessing, it is only because I am too deaf, blind, and faithless to accept it.

Notes

1. Karl Olsson, *Come to the Party* (Waco: Word, 1972), 19.

2. Timothy Keller, *The Reason for God* (New York: Dutton, 2008), 180.

3. Alexander Whyte, *Bible Characters* (Edinburgh: Oliphant, Anderson & Ferrier, 1900), 172.

4. Monica Furlong, *Merton: A Biography* (San Francisco: HarperCollins, 1980), 225.

5. Eugene Peterson, *Leap Over a Wall* (New York: HarperCollins, 1997), 5.

6. Erich Fromm, *To Have or To Be?* (New York: Harper & Row, 1976), 148.

7. Eugene Peterson, *Traveling Light* (Downer's Grove IL: InterVarsity Press, 1982), 57.

Chapter 8

THE FRESH AIR SOCIETY

If someone were to ask you the purpose of the church, what would you say? As I think about my own answer to the question, I can think of several answers that sound true and right.

The purpose of the church is to worship God. How could anyone dispute that claim? Worship is a central part of what the church does and is.

The purpose of the church is to minister to people who are hurting. We all remember Jesus' mandate to take care of "the least of these," so a strong case could be made for this answer too. The church is a cadre of compassionate caregivers.

The purpose of the church is to proclaim the good news of Jesus Christ to a searching world. This answer is true too. The church does exist to declare a message: God was in Christ, reconciling the world to himself.

The purpose of the church is to teach and train people in the way of Jesus. Who can deny the importance of the educational component of the church? The church does exist to make disciples and to teach people a radically different way to live.

The purpose of the church is to be a community of people who love each other. True again, and indisputable. The church does exist as a loving community, and Christians are called to bear one another's burdens.

Any one of those answers would have to be considered correct. But, while they are technically correct, they don't quite get to the heart of the church's primary task. I think the best and truest answer to the question about the purpose of the church is this one: *The purpose of the church is to give forth the scent of grace.*

During a British conference on comparative religions years ago, scholars from around the world debated what, if anything, was unique to Christianity. Was it the incarnation? The resurrection? What sets Christianity apart from other religions? Informed of the discussion, C. S. Lewis answered unequivocally that the unique contribution of Christianity is grace.

The conferees debated that idea at length and eventually agreed with it. The notion of unconditional, no-strings-attached love goes against the grain of conventional thinking and conventional religion. The Buddhists have their eight-fold path. The Hindus have their doctrine of karma. The Jews have their covenant obligations. The Muslims have their strict code of laws. Only the Christian gospel dares to say, "God loves you before you do one religious act, and God loves you most when you deserve it least."

Not only is that the unique contribution of Christianity to the world, but it is also the unique contribution of the church to society. Gordon McDonald once wrote, "The world can do almost anything as well as, or better, than the church. You need not be a Christian to build houses, feed the hungry, or heal the sick. There is only one thing the world cannot do. It cannot offer grace."[1]

That's why the church exists—to embody grace, teach grace, revel in grace. When we get together at church, we do so to celebrate the good news we have all heard and received. Church is where we go to kick up our heels and do the jitterbug together.

The Scent of Grace

I still remember a trip I took through a subdivision south of Houston years ago. South Bend was a large subdivision of expensive houses not far from where we lived, but I felt like I was driving through a ghost town that afternoon as I drove through its streets. The elementary school in South Bend was boarded up. Of the hundreds of houses there, a car sat in only three driveways. The rest of the homes were shuttered and lifeless. No children played in the yards or rode their bikes in the streets. In fact, there was no noticeable life at all. An eerie silence filled the air as I drove through the neighborhood.

I knew what had prompted this sad scene. South Bend sits next to the infamous Brio site where toxic waste was buried years earlier. The families who moved into the subdivision had no idea their new houses stood next to a burial ground for poisonous waste. Then people started getting strange diseases, pregnant women started having a startling number of miscarriages, and it became obvious that something was terribly wrong. When the toxic waste was discovered next to South Bend, families exited in droves. They filed lawsuits and reached settlements. But South Bend as a community was gone forever, killed by the toxic waste buried beside it.

There are days when I think all of us are like those people who lived in South Bend. We're living in a toxic culture, breathing poisonous fumes, and we don't even know it. Or maybe we *do* know it, but the fumes are killing us and our children and grandchildren. The only antidote to those fumes is the scent of grace. Church is where people can go to breathe fresh air.

I think the church's main purpose is giving forth that scent because, when I read the Gospels, I see grace as central to the life and ministry of Jesus. If it is true that the church is the body of Christ in the world, shouldn't it do what Jesus did when he was here in bodily form? Shouldn't we in the church do precisely what Jesus did? Everywhere Jesus went, he left the lingering scent of grace in his wake.

I think of Zacchaeus, who was probably having a mid-life crisis before anyone even knew what that was. Zacchaeus was rich, successful, and miserable. He knew there had to be more to life than he was experiencing. So, one day, in a self-forgetting act reminiscent of David's dance in the street, he threw his image out the window and climbed a sycamore tree, hoping to catch a glimpse of this prophet he had heard so much about. What happened next was amazing. Jesus stopped under that tree, called Zacchaeus by name, and said he would like to stay at his house that day. Whatever happened at that meeting changed Zacchaeus's life, and he vowed to become a giver instead of a taker. The story doesn't say what Zaccheus served Jesus to eat, but one thing is clear: the delicious scent of grace permeated the house that day.

I think of the woman with the long hair, tears on her cheeks, and jar of perfume in her hand. She poured the perfume on Jesus' feet and then soaked them with her tears as well. Simon the Pharisee, who was hosting the party, commented that this encounter proved Jesus wasn't a prophet after all. No respectable prophet would hang out with a woman like this. That prompted Jesus to tell a story about two men who owed a debt—one a large debt and one a small one. Both debtors were forgiven, Jesus said, so which would be the most grateful? Naturally, the one who had been forgiven the biggest debt. So, too, Jesus said, with this situation. This woman had many sins, but her love was great too. Lingering there in Simon's house was not only the aroma of that woman's expensive perfume. There was also the unmistakable scent of grace.

I think of Simon Peter, sick with guilt and regret after denying Jesus three times. Then one morning he was fishing by himself when he caught a glimpse of a familiar figure walking on the shore. It looked remarkably like Jesus, but that was impossible because Peter knew he was dead. Still, Peter couldn't contain his curiosity and excitement and swam to shore to see for himself. He discovered, to his amazement, that it was Jesus! What happened next changed his life forever. Jesus gave him the opportunity to affirm his faith and allegiance—not once, not twice, but three times. Then the two of them enjoyed breakfast together on the beach, and that aroma wafting across the water wasn't just the smell of fish frying. It was also the life-changing scent of sweet, sweet grace.

I think of those hardened soldiers who drove the nails in Jesus' hands. Those men must have been cruel, crass, and insensitive, but in the midst of evil, Jesus spoke words of forgiveness, asking God to forgive the soldiers because they didn't really know what they were doing. If those soldiers had even one ounce of humanity left in them, they knew they were being loved in the midst of their sin. There at the foot of that cross, mingled with the stench of blood and sweat, was the scent of grace that had followed Jesus all through his life and stayed with him even in his death.

The list of examples could go on and on, but you get the picture. Everywhere Jesus went, the scent of grace followed him. Think of the woman at the well. Think of Mary and Martha, the calling of the Twelve, the healing of sick people, Jesus' love for children, or his consistent concern for the last, the least, and the lost. What was Jesus' purpose? To bring grace into a toxic world.

That is why it is our task too. Those of us who claim to be the body of Christ are grace-givers in a world where people have to breathe toxic fumes every day. It is not an easy task, and, frankly, we're not very good at it. We're not Jesus, and we're not particularly grace-full, but at least we know our marching orders. Surprisingly, we sometimes exude grace in a grace-less world and actually do what Jesus did.

When we do, it is because we are living squarely in the middle of 1 Corinthians 13, Paul's famous "love chapter." That chapter shows us how sinful people with widely differing personalities and gifts can work together to be the body of Christ. That chapter shows us how to be bearers and sharers of grace.

A Concert of Grace

When you read Paul's correspondence with the Corinthian church, it is obvious that the people there had more than their share of problems. One of those problems was a contentious spirit that divided them into factions. One faction in the Corinthian church claimed to be followers of Apollos. Another faction followed Peter. A third faction followed Paul. They were also divided over the issue of spiritual gifts— which ones were important and which were not. Evidently, the Corinthian church was overrun with Christians who claimed their faction was the truest expression of faith and their particular gift was the one most needed.

In his first letter to those Christians, Paul addressed the issues before finally coming to his solution to their problem in chapter 13.

Whenever I read the "love chapter," I can almost picture the people Paul addressed because I see them in my own church today.

Over in one corner of the Corinthian church there must have been a group we could call the *Enthusiasts*. These were the emotional ones, the tongues-speakers, the ones on fire for God. The word "enthusiasm" comes from the Greek "*en theos*," which means "in God." These people in the Corinthian church were filled with God and emotion. They probably whispered among themselves after the morning worship service, "You know, if the whole church would get enthused we just might accomplish something for the Lord. We need some life around this place." The *Enthusiasts* believed the church is supposed to be an exciting community.

In another corner of that church there must have been a group we could call the *Intellects*. They had their Bibles and commentaries and theology books. They looked over at the *Enthusiasts* and said, "There is certainly a place for emotion in the Christian faith, but real Christianity has to do with the mind. These people who are emotion-centered are too unstable to be the real church." The *Intellects* believed the church is supposed to be a learning community.

In another corner of the church there must have been a group we could call the *Mystics*. After the service, they gathered and talked among themselves and said, "It's important to be enthused and to be intellectual, but neither of those qualities captures the essence of Christianity. The essence of Christianity is a faith that comes through prayer, silence, and worship. Our church needs depth and people with a real and personal relationship with God. When our people experience God personally, we will be able to move mountains." The *Mystics* believed the church is supposed to be a reflective community.

In the fourth corner of the church there must have been a group we could call the *Workers*. They huddled after the morning service and said among themselves, "We're just ordinary people, and, frankly, we can't get into that other stuff. We're just not that emotional or intellectual or mystical. We're people who simply want to do something tangible for Jesus. What really counts is action. Give us a class to teach or a sick person to visit because faith without works is dead." The

Workers believed the church is supposed to be an action-oriented community.

Listen to Paul's words to those four groups in the Corinthian church: "If I speak in the tongues of mortals and of angels [the *Enthusiasts*] but do not have love, I am a noisy gong or a clanging cymbal. If I have prophetic powers, and understand all mysteries and all knowledge [the *Intellects*], and if I have all faith so as to remove mountains [the *Mystics*] but do not have love, I am nothing. If I give away all my possessions, and if I hand over my body so that I may boast [the *Workers*], but do not have love, I gain nothing" (1 Cor 13:1-3).

Do you see what Paul has done? He has addressed all four of those groups in the Corinthian church and shown them that without *agape*, their way is inadequate. The *Enthusiasts*, the *Intellects*, the *Mystics*, and the *Workers* all have a role to play, but their role must be undergirded by the kind of love Paul describes in 1 Corinthians 13.

What had happened there in Corinth? I think it must have been something like what has happened in your church and mine. Some of the people were floundering and then they found new life in Christ, got excited about their discovery, and became the *Enthusiasts*. Some were confused and groping for truth until they found the ultimate truth in Jesus and became the *Intellects*. Some in Corinth were struggling to experience God, but then they did experience God through prayer, silence, and worship and became the *Mystics*. Some of those people felt empty and useless until they found something of eternal significance, put their hand to the proverbial plow, and became the *Workers*.

The truth is, of course, that we need all of those groups in the church. Where would we be without the *Enthusiasts* who remind us that joy is the most infallible proof of the presence of God in our lives? Where would we be without the *Intellects* challenging us to love God with our minds? Where would we be without the *Mystics* reminding us to experience God personally? Where would we be without the *Workers* building houses, teaching classes, and going on mission trips? We would be infinitely poorer as churches without each of those groups.

What we must know is that those four groups will never see Christianity exactly the same. A line from *The Music Man* says, "We can stand nose to nose for days and days and never see eye to eye." Those groups have different ways of approaching life and God, and they will never completely see eye to eye. But they truly need each other to be a whole body—which is precisely what Paul said in First Corinthians.

What we all need to do, Paul said, is to have a God-like love and respect for one another. Let the *Enthusiasts, Intellects, Mystics,* and *Workers* meld into one harmonious body through the power of *agape.* Let them draw together around this attitude: "Love is patient; love is kind; love is not envious or boastful or arrogant or rude. It does not insist on its own way; it is not irritable or resentful; it does not rejoice in wrongdoing, but rejoices in the truth. It bears all things, believes all things, hopes all things, endures all things" (1 Cor 13:4-7).

This is where it all finally curves around to the church as a community that exudes the scent of grace. The church gives forth that scent by being a model of grace inside itself. Yes, the church shows grace to those outside, those in the world, but the church serves primarily as a model of grace by showing the world that people who are different can do wonderful things together. The *Enthusiasts,* the *Intellects,* the *Mystics,* and the *Workers* might never see life and God eye to eye, but that matters little to them. They have all received the touch of God's grace, blessed by a love they neither earned nor deserved, and they are going to let *agape* rule the day. They love one another . . . regardless. In their differences, they choose to be a concert of grace— to each other and to the world.

Growing in Grace

At least, that's the way it's *supposed* to work. We can all recall churches where that concert of grace became a cacophony of strident voices all claiming to know the truth. Church in theory is great; church in practice is messy and less than perfect.

Paul was trying to pull the Corinthians into a deeper experience of grace. He wanted them to "grow in grace." It is fair to say, I think, that church is a breeding ground for grace. Live long enough in the church and one of two things will happen: you either despair or become grace-full. Church is where we go to grow up into a life of grace.

We're all destined to grow old, but growing up is optional. I remember all too well the pain of receiving my AARP card in the mail. I was still a young guy, not quite fifty years old. I was playing tennis, strumming the guitar, lifting weights three times a week. And they sent *me* an AARP card. The American Association of Retired People. I knew what those people were like. They were old, worn out, with one foot in the grave. I was very young and vigorous, full of life. But there it was, my very own AARP card. No one had prepared me for the shock of that day, but now I've made peace with it and resigned myself to it. Unless we have a tragic accident or disease, we are all destined to grow old.

But we're not all destined to grow up. It is not automatic that we will become wise, real, gracious, or patient in our suffering. The fruits of the Spirit are optional. Church, for all its flaws and sins, is one of the tools God uses to grow us up. Church is the nest in which we learn how to grow up and fly.

Think of a few of the truths we learn by living together at church:

- We learn that we don't always get our way. Sometimes we have to give in and accede to the desires of others.
- We learn that others can do some things better than we can, so we are grateful for their giftedness.
- We learn that we are responsible for carrying our weight. We teach the class, sing in the choir, serve on the committee, or show up for the worship service because that act is part of our commitment, and we are learning to be responsible.
- We learn that love involves receiving as well as giving, and we humble ourselves and receive the help people bring us when we're hurting or grieving.
- We learn that money is for giving, not hoarding. We give regularly and sometimes sacrificially as a reminder that we are stewards of God's good gifts.

- We learn that the church is far from perfect and we'd better accept imperfect people, for we are also imperfect.
- We learn that the gospel of Jesus Christ has a lot more depth and substance than most of the self-help treatises so popular in our culture.

If the church is really the body of Christ, what we learn above all these things is grace. We learn to accept people who approach life and God in a different way than we do. Even further, we learn to *embrace* and *be grateful* for people who approach life and God in a different way. At church, we learn that what Jesus gave all those people he encountered in the Gospels is what we give our brothers and sisters in Christ.

I began this chapter by listing five possible, and accurate, purposes of the church. That list actually came from old seminary notes in my files. We learned in one of our classes that the church exists to perform five functions: worship, ministry, evangelism, education, and fellowship. Those five functions are mirrored in the purposes of the church I mentioned at the beginning of the chapter. As I said, you could make a case for any one of them as the best purpose of the church.

However, I think they must all be colored by the scent of grace, or none of them will happen. Any one of those five functions is doomed to fail if it is not done with grace by grateful people. Without the scent of grace, worship is dry and legalistic. Without the scent of grace, ministry is forced and contrived. Without the scent of grace, evangelism comes across as formulaic and "salesman-like." Without the scent of grace, education is boring and predictable. Without the scent of grace, fellowship is shallow and fake. In short, without the scent of grace, we do the things a church is supposed to be doing, but none of it is joyful, and none of it is effective.

An old story about Mark Twain gets to the heart of the problem. The story goes that his wife, in an attempt to get him to stop cursing, came in one day and unleashed a torrent of curse words in his presence. She wanted him to hear how vile and unbecoming cursing sounds. Mark Twain reportedly withstood her barrage of swearing and then calmly commented that while she certainly knew the words, she didn't know the music at all.

It is possible for those of us in the church to know the words, but not the music. We can do our worship, ministry, evangelism, education, and fellowship with uncommon devotion, but unless we do them with a spirit of grace, they have little effect. Without the sweet harmony of grace, church falls apart. That is who we are because that is who Jesus was. We are *his* body, and the more we get in step with him, the closer we come to fulfilling our calling.

My *AARP Magazine* arrived this week with a message appropriate for all of us, but especially for those of us trying to be the scent of grace in the church. A little blurb in the magazine said, "At 50, you know that the kids grow up fast. At 75, you know that the grandkids grow up fast. At 100, you know that no one ever really grows up."

It's true: No one ever really grows up into the fullness of Christ. We will never be as grace-full as Jesus, but that's the direction in which we're supposed to head. Bringing the scent of grace into a grace-less world is, above all else, the purpose of the church.

Note

1. Quoted in Philip Yancey, *What's So Amazing about Grace?* (Grand Rapids: Zondervan, 1997), 15.

Chapter 9

NOTES TO CHURCH LEADERS

My father was the most positive person I've ever known. One of his brothers captured Dad perfectly when he told me one day, "Travis can always find the bluebird on the dung heap." That is true. Dad had the amazing capacity to look into a pile of thorns and find the rose.

When he discovered he had kidney cancer and had to make regular trips to the hospital to get interferon treatments, he turned those trips into adventures. He made friends with the doctors and nurses at the hospital and looked forward to seeing them. He and Mom enjoyed the ride home, noticed the beauty along the way, and stopped at one of their favorite restaurants if Dad felt up to it. Leave it to Dad to turn cancer treatments into joyful excursions.

When the doctors eventually informed him that the treatments weren't working and that he had only a few months to live, Dad once again saw something good in their grim report. Mom had died suddenly in her sleep one night in the midst of these cancer treatments, so Dad broke the doctor's news to me by saying that he was going to get to be with Mom. Death for him would be swallowed up in the victory of a reunion with his wife and best friend. Had the Apostle Paul not beaten him to the punch, Dad might have written, "I have learned to be content with whatever I have" (Phil 4:11b).

He also had the habit of writing encouraging notes to my brother, sister, and me. He wrote one-liners and left them on the kitchen table for us or slipped them onto our bedroom dressers. I would come home from school and find a note that said, "JB—We're proud of you, Dad" or "Good job today" or even "Bar-B-Q in the fridge." We all knew one thing for certain: if Dad left us a note, it was going to be positive and uplifting. All three of us could have compiled a book of those little notes Dad left around the house for us. All three of us, I think, are still encouraged by them today.

What I'm going to say in this chapter is in the spirit of my father's notes. I want to offer words of hope and encouragement to those who lead churches—pastors and other staff members who have, I think, an increasingly difficult task. It is not easy to be a church leader these days (if it ever was!), and we need all the encouragement we can get. I offer these notes not because I'm an authority who knows things you don't know, but because I know how much it means to find a friendly note on the kitchen table. Think of these words as notes placed on the table so you can get a shot of joy as you live and tell the good news.

On the Kitchen Table

I offer you ten quick notes of encouragement:

Claim the blessing. People might assume that pastors and church staff members are among the select few who enjoy the blessing of God. They might assume that those of us who are "called into the ministry" get the blessing as a part of our call. Those people make a wrong assumption. It has been my experience and observation that many of us who labor in the vineyard of the Lord are actually unblessed. Karl Olsson agrees with me:

> It would be unscientific and unfair to conclude that all or most clergyman are unblessed children who seem to compensate for their lack of favor by working terribly hard at being good. But if I draw on my own experience, I have to conclude that many ministers I know and many so-called "dedicated laymen" are unblessed. They may deserve a goat and a party, but they lack the security to ask for it. Hence they wear themselves out in a tiresome and unrewarding round of activities. They stay near the father and carry out their

work under his nose, but they are never very happy, and when anyone is too happy around them, they feel frustrated and envious.[1]

The notion that we church leaders automatically have the blessing of God on our lives is false. Many of us feel unblessed, worn out, and frustrated. We have the elder brother and Michal syndromes. The best thing we could do for ourselves, our families, and our churches is to do what Jacob did when he wrestled with the Lord at Peniel: not let go of God until we receive the blessing (see Gen 32:26).

There is incredibly good news for all of us men and women of the cloth: We don't have to do one religious thing to get God's blessing. We don't have to increase attendance at church, have a budget surplus, entice hordes of people to join, solve everyone's problems, mediate everyone's disputes, or answer everyone's questions about the Bible. We don't have to hit a home run every time we step into the pulpit or say just "the right thing" at funerals and weddings. We don't have to smile, succeed, shake everyone's hands, serve on denominational committees, stand tall in the midst of every conflict, remain stoic at all times, or sacrifice our humanity to protect our ministerial image.

Granted, we might need to do some of those things to get the blessing of the people in our church. In fact, if we're unduly concerned about those things, it is probably because we want their blessing desperately. But, praise God, we don't have to do one thing on that list to get God's blessing. We already have all the love and delight God can give us.

For your sake and the sake of the people who love you most, claim that blessing and live out of the center of it. You need to hear what Jesus heard, and it will make all the difference in your ministry: you are God's beloved son or daughter, and with you God is well pleased.

Be an agent of grace. Sometimes we ministers get confused and forget who we are—especially when even people in our church call us by different names and assign us different roles.

Several years ago, I heard a funny, and supposedly true, story about a kindergarten teacher in California in the 1970s. This was back in the days when parents in California gave their offspring wild and unusual names like "Dweezil" and "Moon Unit," so the teacher expected some of her students to have strange names. But one little boy had the most bizarre name the teacher had ever heard.

The school had asked the parents to put a name tag on their children so the teacher would know each child's name when he or she got off the bus. When this little boy stepped off the bus, the teacher was shocked to see the name on his tag. There in bold letters, so it could not be missed, was the name "Fruitstand." The teacher was aghast at the insensitivity of parents who would brand a child with such a name. She decided to give him extra attention and spent the day trying to affirm and encourage little Fruitstand. With a name like that, the teacher figured, this little boy needed all of the affirmation he could get.

Throughout the day, the teacher went out of her way to check on the little boy: "Fruitstand, do you need some water?" "Fruitstand, are you doing okay?" "Fruitstand, do you need any help?"

Later on that first day of school, one of the other kindergarten teachers remarked how helpful it was to have the children's names on the tags and also, on the other side, the names of the places where the bus would let them off.

A light clicked on in the teacher's head. She rushed to the little boy to verify what she suspected. She flipped his name tag over and, sure enough, on the other side of "Fruitstand" was the name "Anthony."

I laugh at that story every time I tell it, but I think it says something about the identity of those of us who call ourselves ministers. Just who are we anyway? Depending on who you ask, one person in the church wants us to be Spellbinding Orator. Another would call us Bible Scholar. Another would have us be Institutional Guru. Another would dub us Great Fundraiser. Another Rescuer of Our Dying Church. There are countless people, both within and without the church, ready to call us "Fruitstand."

Those are not our names. On the other side of those name tags is our real name: Agent of Grace. We are to be agents of grace in the pulpit, in committee meetings, in hospital rooms, at weddings and funerals. Everywhere we go, we should try to give off the scent of grace, and people feel freer and more affirmed because we were with them. We are to do for people exactly what Jesus did for Zacchaeus, the woman who anointed him with perfume, Simon Peter, the soldiers at the cross, and everyone else he met.

As you move out into the world today to do your ministry, laugh and celebrate and be an agent of grace to all you meet. That is who you are because that is who Jesus was.

Get a life. I say this not in the haughty, critical way people in our culture usually say it. I say it as a reminder that your life is bigger than the church. Your life is more than church business, attendance and offering totals, sermon titles, hospital visits, and upset deacons. Or, at least, your life *should* be more than those things. You have a life, for God's sake, or, if you don't, please get one.

Take your kids to the zoo this afternoon. Head to the tennis courts and hit some balls. Take your husband or wife to a movie. Start collecting stamps or old radios. Go to the park and compose a song. Do something, anything, that will remind you that life is more than church, church worries, and church people.

I have often said that Thursday has saved my ministry. Thursday is my day off, and it's the day I use to remind myself that I have a life. I begin Thursday by reading the paper and having several cups of coffee. Sherry and I eat breakfast together, and then I head to the tennis court to play a rousing game of doubles with "the old guys." Then we four tennis pros go to a local bagels shop, drink more coffee, and talk about some of the incredible shots we hit that day.

After tennis, Sherry and I go grocery shopping, which we actually enjoy. We typically eat out somewhere and then go home to take a nap. After the nap, we might go to the bookstore or a movie, putter in the yard, make our soup of the week, or take a walk in a nearby park. By the time we make it to the supper table, we're hungry but relaxed. We might read a while after supper, and then drift off to bed fairly early.

Most Thursdays, I don't go to the church or even think about the church. I think about my backhand, what we're going to buy at the grocery store, which restaurant we want to try for lunch, what new book I need to purchase, and which soup we will cook for the week. It's all so normal and ordinary that it's life renewing. It reminds me that I have a life and that my life is bigger than what happens at church. If, heaven help us, something goes wrong and the people at the church decide my services are no longer required, I think I would be fine. Hurt, maybe. But fine. Because the church is not me, and it's not my life.

It is one of the true paradoxes of church life that staff people who don't live and breathe the church are the ones who serve and lead the best. There's something attractive about anyone who has a life and enjoys living it.

Be true to your calling. Just because you and I are church leaders doesn't mean our ministries have any similarities. Every ministry is a unique adventure, and no two people minister the same way.

I had to smile when I read the following confession from Robert Capon:

> I have never done an honest day's work as a clergyman. In fact, I hate, despise, and avoid at least half the things clergypersons are supposed to do. I love preaching, celebrating the Eucharist, teaching, and counseling; so I have done those things just for the joy of it. I am also moderately fond of administration (which I delight in doing as quickly as possible), and I am more than a little enamored of ecclesiastical politics (which I have pursued with relish, if not always with success). But I have little love for writing newsletters, attending other people's meetings, paying house calls, or visiting in the hospital; so (since they are no fun), I have done as little of them as I could get away with.[2]

When I look over his likes and dislikes, I realize that, though we are kindred spirits theologically, Capon and I have different ministries. Like him, I love preaching and leading worship, but unlike him, I don't enjoy teaching or counseling. He is moderately fond of administration; I'm not fond of it at all. He is enamored of ecclesiastical politics; I have no interest in it whatsoever. He dislikes visiting in the hospital, while I enjoy that part of being a pastor. He plays to his strengths, and I play to mine and, in the best of all worlds, the kingdom of God gets nudged along because both of us are being true to ourselves and our calling.

The shape of your ministry is unique. Go with your strengths. Use the gifts God has bestowed upon you. If you're a writer, write. If you're an administrator, administer. If you're a counselor, counsel. Be true to your gifts and calling. The kingdom will benefit, and you will be a happier minister because you're doing "your thing."

Follow Jesus. My bookshelves are lined with books about leadership. Through the years, I've bought many books written to help business leaders become successful. Several years ago, I stopped buying those books because I realized they weren't addressed to me at all. As I said, they were addressed to business leaders wanting to become successful, and I fail to meet both of those criteria. I'm not a business leader, and I'm not supposed to be successful in the way those books define success. I got off of the leadership and success bandwagons and crawled back on the Jesus bandwagon.

The bad news about that is that most churches today seem to want leaders who are still on the leadership and success bandwagons. The church is taking its cue from the business world and looking for leaders who could "run" big companies. Eugene Peterson writes,

> I am in conversation right now with a dozen or so men and women who are waiting to be called by a congregation. And I am having the depressing experience of reading congregational descriptions of what these churches want in a pastor. With hardly an exception they don't want pastors at all—they want managers of their religious company. They want a pastor they can follow so they won't have to bother with following Jesus anymore.[3]

One reason many of us get discouraged is that we're trying to play roles we're not supposed to play. We're not managers of a religious company, psychologists, marketing experts, or financial consultants. We're ministers. We're pastors, or ministers of music, youth, children, or outreach. As such, our marching orders are not the same as those given to CEOs of large companies. We're following Jesus, not growth charts, and Jesus offers us wise counsel and the perfect role model for doing our work.

Practice fidelity. Since we're talking about Jesus, let's let him remind us that what we're about is fidelity, not success. By any business criteria you want to use, Jesus was not successful. He alienated the important people of his day. He experienced constant conflict. His best friends misunderstood him. He crashed and burned after three short years of ministry. He ended up crucified as a common criminal. That's not exactly the résumé of a successful person, as the business books depict a successful person. Still, we declare Jesus a whopping success because he was faithful to God all through his life, faithful to God even in his death. Jesus' life reminds us that fidelity is our goal, and fidelity defines our success.

It is entirely possible that you find yourself stuck in what looks to be a most unsuccessful church. You have looked for brilliant, stimulating people in the pews and have nearly decided that there are none. You have been in the church for years, perhaps, and nothing has changed. The church hasn't grown. The people still resist progress of any kind. You wonder, some days, exactly why you stay in this place. Shouldn't you be selling life insurance or real estate? Doesn't a career as a forest ranger look appealing?

Jeff Berryman's novel, *Leaving Ruin*, tells the story of Cyrus Manning, a pastor laboring faithfully in a barren West Texas town. Cyrus wonders, at one point in the book, what most church leaders eventually wonder:

> Is it false, this "call" of mine? Have I missed my life? I'm supposed to be an attorney in New York, probably, or Iowa, or a pilot, or fireman, but not this evangelical, protestant, preacher-teacher thing where old women get ugly and spiteful and old men just go to sleep, and sometimes there's this deep anger that rises because nobody knows what I really am, except maybe Jesus, and what about when it doesn't feel like he's around, either, and maybe it's not too late to go to school again, and make my way the way I want . . . .[4]

I would simply remind us all that we are called to be the scent of grace wherever we happen to serve. If we happen to land in a booming, bustling church that makes us look successful, we're the scent of grace there. If we happen to find ourselves in a dying inner-city church where only a handful of old people show up, we're supposed to be the scent of grace there too. Success, in both places, has nothing to do with the size of the crowd.

There was a time in our church in San Antonio when I preached faithfully for five months and not one person came forward at the end of the service to join our church. For five months I preached as passionately and lovingly as I could with no visible response. There came another five-month span, a few years later, when I preached passionately and lovingly and more than ninety people united with our church. Same preacher, same passion, same style of preaching, but very different results.

When I look back at those two seasons in the life of our church, I am most proud now of the first one. I just kept preaching, kept the faith, knew that the payoff was not people walking an aisle but the joy of keeping on keeping on. We pastors and church leaders are called to a life of fidelity, and if we can accomplish that, we are successful no matter what the numbers say.

Get real. Every Wednesday night at our church, we have supper together at 5:30. Then the children and youth wander off to their activities, and the adults stay in the fellowship hall for a brief time of worship. Almost every week, I get out my guitar and lead a couple of songs, we have a brief devotional thought, and then we have prayer together. The entire service in the fellowship hall lasts less than thirty minutes.

On several occasions, I've tried to phase out the guitar portion of the service, but I always get protests when I do. For some strange reason, people like me strumming the guitar and all of us singing in harmony to old hymns and choruses. I am certain that it is not my accomplished guitar playing that brings the protests. Many pastors preach sermons with three points; I am a pastor who plays songs with three chords. A guitar virtuoso I am not.

So why does the Wednesday night crowd like it when the pastor strums the guitar and sings old songs? My guess is that it makes me real. On Sundays, I'm ecclesiastical and official. I'm the pastor in his black robe pontificating from the pulpit, high and holy and lifted up. On Wednesday nights, I'm Jud in his khaki pants strumming the guitar. On Wednesday nights, I eat spaghetti and converse with the folks at our table, then I get my guitar and sing, and then we have prayer requests. It's all casual, relaxed, and real. I'm thinking the appeal of the guitar is really the appeal of a pastor being a normal human being.

I'm sure some church people would rather keep their pastor high and holy and lifted up. There might even be people in my church who wish I would put that silly guitar away and start acting like a dignified pastor. Even so, many seem to like the notion that their pastor is a real human being who eats spaghetti with them and then gets out his old guitar and makes a fool of himself.

There is an old and perhaps apocryphal story about Vince Lombardi, the great coach of the Green Bay Packers. The story goes that one night his wife crawled into bed with him and exclaimed, "God, your feet are cold!" To which he replied, "You can call me Vince in bed."

It helps both the congregation and the staff if we all remember that church leaders are ordinary humans. The more real we are, the more authentic our ministries become. As you move out into your parish this week, take your guitar with you and see what happens.

Hang loose. Church is a breeding ground for stress. Why do we church leaders get anxious at church? Let me count the ways:

• Margaret is upset with you because you failed to visit her mother's third cousin who was in the hospital for two days, and "no one from the church came to see her."
• The youth minister showed a movie at the last lock-in in which some character said a bad word, and now parents wonder what your church is coming to and why you hired such an incompetent person to lead the youth.

- Offerings are down slightly from last year, and people are clamoring for more Sunday school lessons on stewardship.
- The six-week remodeling job on the nursery and preschool area is now entering its fourth month.
- The church people are grumbling that you spend too much time away from the church, and your spouse is grumbling that you spend too much time away from home.
- At the last staff meeting, two staff members snipped at each other, and you sense a storm is brewing.
- It's Thursday, and the sermon for Sunday is not coming together.

That's just the start of the list. When you walk into your church every morning, you walk into a stress factory.

What shall we do? How about "hang loose and keep it all in perspective"? How about "this too shall pass and will be replaced by other equally irritating issues"? How about "I refuse to be stoned to death by popcorn and will lift my eyes to the hills from whence cometh my help"?

Easier said than done, I know, but it is probably true that the best gift we give our churches is our attitude—an attitude that refuses to sweat the small stuff so we can all keep our eyes trained on the big stuff.

Shake free. One of the biggest enemies of effective ministry, I have come to believe, is a creeping busyness that eventually overwhelms us with things to do. My daughter and her husband had bamboo growing in their backyard, which was nice until it started to spread. It was about to take over the yard until my son-in-law took the bull by the horns and attacked it. He got rid of all the bamboo, planted new grass, and the backyard was restored.

Most ministers end up with more than their share of ecclesiastical bamboo. It sneaks into our schedules almost unnoticed. One prayer at the Rotary Club. One preaching assignment at the nursing home. One meeting with a committee. One class party. One youth fellowship. They all seem so benign and simple, but, taken together, they wind up being bamboo that overtakes us and keeps us preoccupied with the nonessential.

Writing this book has been an exercise in getting rid of the bamboo in my ministry. Once I knew I was going to write the book, I cleared out space to make it a priority. I decided to focus on writing and preaching for several months and have been able to do that most days. I'm typing this right now at a Krispy Kreme on a laptop I bought for $200 on eBay. Many afternoons, I escape the church office and head either to Krispy Kreme or Starbucks to write. For two or three hours, I sip coffee and write on the laptop, and it has been a fun and rewarding time for me. It has also shown me that I have more time available to me most days than I realize.

In *The Contemplative Pastor*, Eugene Peterson tells of the time when he needed physical therapy three times a week for back trouble. He said he was able to do the therapy for weeks, and no one at the church seemed to miss him. That has been my experience too. I take my laptop and settle into one of those coffee places to write, and the church seems to do just fine, thank you very much. It is highly probable that I am not as indispensable as I think. Neither, I am guessing, are you.

Convene the party. If the good news becomes good again in contemporary American culture, it will be because church leaders recover the wonder of the gospel and become contagious. It will be because pastors who have long labored under the burden of religion drop it, recover the lightness of grace, and start to preach good news. It will be because ministers of music, often caught in the crossfire of opposing musical styles, start to feel the good news in their bones and let their music reflect it. It will be because ministers of youth, tired of playing games with kids or hitting them over the head with "relevant Bible studies," get an injection of good news and then grow excited about their youth knowing the good news too. Though I never underestimate the power of the laity, I doubt that the good news will ever become good again if those of us in church leadership roles don't lead the way.

Please convene the party in your church. In your choir. In your youth group. In Vacation Bible School. Let the wonderful grace of God free you from the burden of religion so that, like David, you can dance in the streets. Of course, some Michals will chide you for your frivolity. But dance any way, and kill the fatted calf and have your party. If God is for you, working in your life and ministry and infusing you with daily strength, who or what can possibly defeat you?

Simple Reminders

As I glance back over what I just wrote, I doubt that you learned one new thing as you read those notes. I'm not particularly dismayed by that because I simply wanted to do for you what my father did for me when he left his cryptic notes on the kitchen table. I wanted to encourage you, give you a shot of energy, and assure you that someone else has been where you are and felt what you feel.

Probably, too, I wrote those notes as much to encourage myself as to encourage you. As my dad got older, I noticed he would leave other notes on the kitchen table—intended not for his children but for himself. They would say "pick up cleaning" or "take out trash" or "get pills." As he got older, he became a bit forgetful, so he wrote himself those notes to make sure he did what he was supposed to do.

After all of these years as a pastor, I need to do that too. I need to write myself notes so I will remember who I am and what I promised to be and do. As I enter the final years of my ministry, I want to finish strong.

As we head toward the finish line of this book, I want to finish it strong too and remind us of one verse and one truth that give us the motivation we need to live for God. This one truth alone makes the good news good again, so we dare not forget it.

Notes

1. Karl Olsson, *Come to the Party* (Waco TX: Word, 1972), 30.

2. Robert Capon, *Health, Money, and Love & Why We Don't Enjoy Them* (Grand Rapids: Eerdmans, 1990), 143.

3. Eugene Peterson and Marva Dawn, *The Unnecessary Pastor* (Grand Rapids: Eerdmans, 2000), 4.

4. Jeff Berryman, *Leaving Ruin* (Orange CA: New Leaf Books, 2002), 42.

Chapter 10

FIRST THINGS FIRST

When I was growing up in that church in Houston, we had a tried-and-true formula for restoring spiritual passion. As I mentioned earlier, every year we had a revival. We brought in an evangelist who was a lot more rambunctious and entertaining than our pastor. We also brought in a singer who dressed in bright clothes and sported a bouffant hairdo.

We designated one night of the week as "Pizza Night," one night as "Hot Dog Night," and inevitably we had a "Pack-the-Pew Night." Our revivals typically lasted a week, and by the time they were over, we all felt energized and guilty. We stayed energized for several weeks, but the guilt lingered much longer. By the next year, we were all spiritually flat and ready to be revived again.

As I look back over what I have written so far, it strikes me that this is a book about revival. Not the kind of revival we had in our church in Houston, but revival nonetheless. The revivals from years ago were loud, emotional, and aimed at sinners. The kind of revival I've been writing about is quiet, personal, and aimed at Christians. I'm envisioning a personal revival where people who have been Christians for a long time recover the wonder of the gospel, become one of the blessed, and start to experience the joy of their salvation. I've aimed this entire book in that one direction: to help longtime Christians experience the good news of the gospel.

I have called this chapter "First Things First" because I want to make sure we understand what can enable us to recover the wonder of the gospel and what can spark a revival in our hearts. That can happen only when we get an inkling of God's love for us. Everything starts with the unconditional, sacrificing, searching love of God. Without an awareness of how much God delights in us, our attempts at personal revival are as sounding brass or a tinkling cymbal.

No More Trading Stamps

There was a time, not many years ago, when people collected trading stamps. Shoppers received them at grocery stores. For so many dollars spent on groceries, they got so many trading stamps in return. Then those shoppers could take the trading stamps home, paste them in a book, and eventually redeem them for merchandise. Sherry and I were trading stamp people when we first got married and occasionally carried our trading stamp books to the redemption store and then hauled home our prize—a new can opener, perhaps, or a lamp for the living room.

Most of the religion practiced in America today is a trading stamp kind of religion. We Christians collect our religious trading stamps and hope to redeem them someday at the heavenly redemption store. We pray, worship, tithe, witness, serve on church committees, study the Bible, and so on, with the fond hope that we will win God's approval and get an eternal prize. We also hope God will notice how quickly our stamp books are filling up and see fit to reward us now. We want an eternal prize, for sure, but an occasional prize in the here and now would be nice too.

For many people, then, the Christian life is a sincere attempt to collect those stamps and redeem them, both now and in eternity. The problem with trading stamp religion is twofold: first, it has nothing to do with who Jesus was and what Jesus taught, and, second, it is awfully bad news. Think a moment about each of those drawbacks.

First, trading stamp religion is the antithesis to who Jesus was and what Jesus taught. Trading stamp religion is actually an old way of coming at God. It was, in fact, the religion of the Pharisees. They had rules and laws to obey, and every time they obeyed, they could paste another stamp in their books and feel proud of themselves. As you remember, Jesus lambasted this approach to God and saved his harshest criticism for these men. You can't read the Gospels without realizing that Jesus wanted nothing to do with trading stamp religion.

Second, trading stamp religion is bad news. There is nothing delightful about keeping track of your good works and trying hard to please a demanding deity. Inevitably, that kind of religion produces people like the Pharisees—moral, antiseptic, uptight rule-keepers trying to look better than the people around them. When we survey the current religious scene in our country, isn't that what we see? The most zealous Christians seem to be the ones who are the most angry and haughty. Even those of us who know better often fall away from grace and become Pharisees ourselves.

That is why I decided to write this book and why I believe the greatest need in the church today is making the good news good again. We need a revival in the church that goes beyond people walking aisles and getting saved. I'm thinking of a quiet revival where normal, sensible people get sick and tired of bad news religion and collecting their trading stamps and decide to bet their lives on the gospel of grace. They accept the blessing of God on their lives and then start to bless the people around them. This revival wouldn't feel particularly doctrinal or religious, but it would liberate and give life. It would brim with good news.

I think this is where the revival will begin. It will begin quietly in individual people's lives as they realize how much God loves them and how amazing God's grace is. It will begin when individual Christians give up trading stamp religion and embrace the kind of faith described in the little book of 1 John. A sentence in 1 John gives us the ideal motivation for everything we do. It enables us to get our priorities straight and put first things first.

The Motivation Ladder

Before we look at that sentence from 1 John, let's think first about people's possible motivations for relating to God. From bottom to top, the motivation ladder has three rungs:

1. No motivation for relating to God. At the bottom of the ladder is an attitude that ignores or shuns God. For many people, God is simply not a factor in their lives. They're wrapped up in jobs, families, making money, and having fun and don't give much thought to God. Some of them are anti-God, but most are just oblivious to God. For whatever reason, God is not on the radar screen of their lives.

Some of them assuredly will start thinking of God somewhere along the way. Some event—a birth, death, or crisis—will cause them to lift their eyes to the hills and consider issues bigger than the next paycheck or "Monday Night Football." We can only pray that the Hound of Heaven will pursue these people until they have eyes to see and ears to hear the good news.

If they don't? If they never put God on the radar screen of their lives? Then, according to the New Testament, they reside in hell. I have come to see hell not as a repudiation of the good news but as an integral part of it. Hell is part of the good news because it acknowledges God's willingness to let humans be free, free even to go their own way without God if they choose.

Hell is not so much a place as it is a condition. It is the condition of living without God, without grace and forgiveness, without the blessing. I have also come to believe that you don't have to die to go to hell. It can be a present condition, and many people around us have taken up residence there.

But the door to hell locks only from the inside, and anyone who wants to walk out of hell and join the party can do so. I even have the fond hope that some day in eternity, hell will be empty. Perhaps the Hound of Heaven will so relentlessly pursue people that everyone will finally see the light and come home.

The bottom rung on the motivation ladder is no motivation at all. If God is alive and well and changing people's lives, those at this level don't know it.

2. Relating to God out of fear. A step up from no motivation is the desire to love God and serve God out of fear. People on this rung of the ladder see God the way I saw the bully Doyle Jennings. God is critical, fearful, and looking for people to judge. At least people on this rung of the motivational ladder are tuned into God, though. At least they know there is an eternal, transcendent dimension to life.

As I mentioned in chapter 3, much of the fear people have of God comes from the Bible itself. There are frightening passages, as God decrees the destruction of entire cities or demands the stoning of disobedient children. In some parts of Scripture, God is awesome, fearsome, and ready to wreak havoc on sinners.

Yet, the governing word in the Bible has to be Jesus, who says clearly that God *loves* sinners. We are not sinners in the hands of an angry God, after all; we are sinners in the hands of a gracious God. When we settle into this second rung of the motivational ladder, we fail to see that. We have a relationship with God, but it's a relationship of fear and uncertainty.

3. Relating to God out of gratitude. The sentence that gives us the best and highest motivation is 1 John 4:19: "We love because he first loved us." John writes about fear, the second rung on the motivational ladder, and tries to move his readers beyond it: "There is no fear in love, but perfect love casts out fear; for fear has to do with punishment, and whoever fears has not reached perfection in love" (1 John 4:18). Mature faith finally makes it to rung 3 on the motivation ladder where we move beyond fear and relate to God out of gratitude.

We love because he first loved us. Furthermore, we preach, pray, give, study, meditate, bear witness in foreign lands, serve on church committees, love our families, do our jobs, coach our teams, write our books, compose our songs, and bake our bread because he first loved us. Everything we Christians do is in response to the incredible love of God that arrives with no strings attached. God loved us *first*. God is *for* us. Life is one big alleluia of gratitude as a result.

Announcing the Jubilee

One way to think of this quiet revival of grace and gratitude that could take place in our hearts is to go back to the Old Testament and remember the Jubilee. In Leviticus 25, we read the details of the year of Jubilee that the people of Israel were to celebrate every fifty years.

When the people moved into the promised land after forty years of wandering in the wilderness, God prescribed this year of Jubilee as a way for them to keep their priorities straight.

At least four things were supposed to happen during the year of Jubilee. First, all slaves were to be set free. Second, all financial debts were to be cancelled. Third, all land was to be returned to its original owners. Fourth, the year was to be a festive, yearlong break from the routine, a yearlong sabbatical.

In effect, the year of Jubilee was supposed to be a year of starting over. When the slaves were freed, they would get a new lease on life. When those burdened with debt had that debt cancelled, they would get a new lease on life too. When land was returned to its original owners, all of those who had built empires of greed would be stripped of those empires, and equity would be restored. Once those three things were accomplished, the fourth thing would come naturally. Festivity would have been the order of the day.

We can only speculate as to what might happen in our own country should Congress decide to declare a nationwide year of Jubilee. I'm certain that won't be happening any time soon, but if it did, our national Jubilee would do three things for us.

First, it would give us a new understanding of stewardship. We would realize that, ultimately, nothing is ours to keep. One purpose of the original Jubilee was to remind the Israelites that everything was God's: "for the land is mine; with me you are but aliens and tenants" (Lev 25:23). We would sit looser, lighten the grip on our stuff, and see the folly of greed and materialism.

Second, it would give us a new sense of freedom. The original Jubilee was to be a year of emancipation and independence: "And you shall hallow the fiftieth year and you shall proclaim liberty to all its inhabitants" (Lev 25:10). Slaves were freed from their owners, debtors were freed from their creditors, and landowners were freed from their greed. If we had such a year in our own country, we would all remember that freedom comes from being, not having. The Jubilee year would destroy our system for determining status, but wouldn't we all be freer people?

Third, it would give us a joyous feeling of celebration. This sabbatical year was supposed to give the people of Israel a time to remember who they were and to celebrate their heritage. They were to remember God's faithfulness and be glad. If we had this celebration in America, perhaps we would take a year to get reacquainted with our families, go on picnics, write poems, sing songs, and count our blessings together.

Two surprising truths surround the year of Jubilee. For one thing, as far as we can tell, Israel never celebrated it. This is the great unfinished business of the Israelite nation. They never got around to obeying the instructions of Leviticus 25.

The other surprising truth about the Jubilee is that Jesus referred to it when he launched his ministry in his hometown of Nazareth. He stood in the synagogue and read from Isaiah 61: "The Spirit of the Lord is upon me because he has anointed me to bring good news to the poor. He has sent me to proclaim release to the captives and recovery of sight to the blind, to let the oppressed go free, to proclaim the year of the Lord's favor" (Luke 4:18-19).

Biblical scholars agree that Jesus probably referred to the year of Jubilee. It was as if Jesus said to his listeners, "All of the benefits of the year of Jubilee will be realized through me. Though our people have never celebrated it, it is now time to let the Jubilee begin. Through me, you will discover how to best use your life and possessions. Through me, you will get a new sense of freedom. And through me, you will experience a new joy. I am announcing the Jubilee, so let the festivities begin!"

You would think those Jews, schooled in the Old Testament and no doubt familiar with Leviticus 25, would have broken out in a song of praise. But, Luke says, by the time Jesus had finished talking to them, they were filled with rage and wanted to hurl him off a cliff. So much for beginning the Jubilee! His words about the Jubilee fell on deaf, even hostile, ears.

Sadly, they *still* fall on deaf ears. We still have a hard time hearing the good news that Jesus came to embody and announce. The quiet, personal revival I envision in this book is simply a recognition of what that crowd in Nazareth did not recognize. We recognize the good news of Jesus and let that good news get in our bones and make us dance.

Some of you reading this book are tired. You have been in the church all of your life. You have served on committees, drafted church bylaws, planned buildings, taught classes, worked with children and youth, kept the nursery, given thousands of dollars to ministry causes, and survived many a bad sermon. Now you are worn out from a faithful life served in the trenches of your church.

Serving in the trenches of a church can wear anyone out. The "mechanics" of the institutional church can eventually sap your energy and siphon your joy. You can get so caught up in institutional things that you forget spiritual things. I believe the year of Jubilee was intended to prevent this. Just as every week is supposed to have a Sabbath to enable us to restore our perspective and recover our joy, so the people of Israel were supposed to have a Sabbath year every fifty years to enable them to regain the wonder of their relationship to God.

As I said, I doubt we will ever have a year of Jubilee here in our country. But couldn't you and I decide to have a private one? Couldn't we quit pushing so hard and relax into the grace of God? Couldn't we stop and realize how blessed we are? Couldn't we sit looser, laugh harder, and love deeper? Couldn't we declare a personal time of Jubilee so we could recover the wonder of the gospel and bask again in the unmerited delight of God?

I think we could.

And I think we should.

Come to the Party

Several times in this book I've quoted from Karl Olsson's book, *Come to the Party*. He wrote that book nearly forty years ago, but I consider it a book with "staying power" for me. Even now, I occasionally get out that book, flip through its pages, and reread the passages I highlighted.

Olsson was a pastor's son, the unblessed child of an unblessed child, as he describes himself. He became a pastor and then a college and seminary president, but he never felt he had the blessing, never felt free to frolic in God's delight. Then, one day in 1967, he had a Jubilee experience and everything changed:

> Some time in the summer of 1967 I came face to face with the real me and suddenly discovered the simple but overwhelming fact which I had preached and written about for thirty years—that we are justified by faith alone and not by works, "lest any man should boast." What this meant for *me*, quite practically, was that God had already accepted the real *me* in Christ and that it was O.K. to be that *me*. I did not have to overlay that *me* with any sweat-soaked slave shirt of my own. I did not have to be a professional prelate, preacher, president, pundit, professor, Protestant, or anything else to make it with God.[1]

God's delight in Olsson became something more than a concept; it became an experience. He was able to become one of the blessed because he experienced that delight.

In his book, *The Molten Soul*, Gray Temple suggests that we try to imagine the absolute glee God feels for each of us:

> You might conceive of God's joy—indeed God's glee—as God whispers your name eternally within the Godhead. Indeed, if God were to stop that whispering for an instant, you would cease utterly to be. Your very being at this moment is the fruit of God's delight. And your life's highest purpose and deepest joy is to experience and agree with that delight.[2]

It might be a hard picture to imagine, but give it a try. God the Father gleefully whispering your name to the Son and Spirit. God continuously creating you with his delight. God feeling about you the way you feel about the one person you love most in the world. Your purpose being to accept that delight and to live in the light of that unconditional love.

If we could picture God and ourselves that way, we would know why Paul exulted as he did in Romans 8:31. We, too, would sing, "If God feels that way about me, who or what can defeat me?" We would become one of the blessed, and we would start to bless other people as never before.

I close with two questions:

Can you believe the good news is really that good?
If so, isn't it about time you came to the party?

Notes

1. Karl Olsson, *Come to the Party* (Waco TX: Word Books, 1971), 47.
2. Gray Temple, *The Molten Soul* (New York: Church Publishing, 2000), 37.

Other available titles from SMYTH&HELWYS

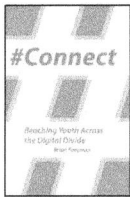

#Connect
Reaching Youth Across the Digital Divide
Brian Foreman

Reaching our youth across the digital divide is a struggle for parents, ministers, and other adults who work with Generation Z—today's teenagers. *#Connect* leads readers into the technological landscape, encourages conversations with teenagers, and reminds us all to be the presence of Christ in every facet of our lives.   *978-1-57312-693-9 120 pages/pb* **$13.00**

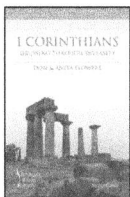

1 Corinthians (Smyth & Helwys Annual Bible Study series)
Growing through Diversity
Don & Anita Flowers

Don and Anita Flowers present this comprehensive study of 1 Corinthians, filled with scholarly insight and dealing with such varied topics as marriage and sexuality, spiritual gifts and love, and diversity and unity. The authors examine Paul's relationship with the church in Corinth as well as the culture of that city to give context to topics that can seem far removed from Christian life today.   *Teaching Guide 978-1-57312-701-1 122 pages/pb* **$14.00**
Study Guide 978-1-57312-705-9 52 pages/pb **$6.00**

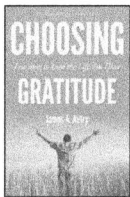

Choosing Gratitude
Learning to Love the Life You Have
James A. Autry

Autry reminds us that gratitude is a choice, a spiritual—not social—process. He suggests that if we cultivate gratitude as a way of being, we may not change the world and its ills, but we can change our response to the world. If we fill our lives with moments of gratitude, we will indeed love the life we have.   *978-1-57312-614-4 144 pages/pb* **$15.00**

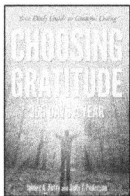

Choosing Gratitude 365 Days a Year
Your Daily Guide to Grateful Living
James A. Autry and Sally J. Pederson

Filled with quotes, poems, and the inspired voices of both Pederson and Autry, in a society consumed by fears of not having "enough"—money, possessions, security, and so on—this book suggests that if we cultivate gratitude as a way of being, we may not change the world and its ills, but we can change our response to the world.   *978-1-57312-689-2 210 pages/pb* **$18.00**

To order call **1-800-747-3016** or visit **www.helwys.com**

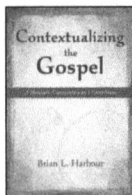

Contextualizing the Gospel
A Homiletic Commentary on 1 Corinthians
Brian L. Harbour

Harbour examines every part of Paul's letter, providing a rich resource for those who want to struggle with the difficult texts as well as the simple texts, who want to know how God's word—all of it—intersects with their lives today.   *978-1-57312-589-5 240 pages/pb* **$19.00**

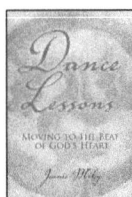

Dance Lessons
Moving to the Beat of God's Heart
Jeanie Miley

Miley shares her joys and struggles a she learns to "dance" with the Spirit of the Living God.   *978-1-57312-622-9 240 pages/pb* **$19.00**

A Divine Duet
Ministry and Motherhood
Alicia Davis Porterfield, ed.

Each essay in this inspiring collection is as different as the mother-minister who wrote it, from theologians to chaplains, inner-city ministers to rural-poverty ministers, youth pastors to preachers, mothers who have adopted, birthed, and done both.

978-1-57312-676-2 146 pages/pb **$16.00**

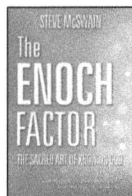

The Enoch Factor
The Sacred Art of Knowing God
Steve McSwain

The Enoch Factor is a persuasive argument for a more enlightened religious dialogue in America, one that affirms the goals of all religions—guiding followers in self-awareness, finding serenity and happiness, and discovering what the author describes as "the sacred art of knowing God."   *978-1-57312-556-7 256 pages/pb* **$21.00**

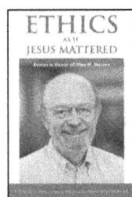

Ethics as if Jesus Mattered
Essays in Honor of Glen H. Stassen
Rick Axtell, Michelle Tooley, Michael L. Westmoreland-White, eds.

Ethics as if Jesus Mattered will introduce Stassen's work to a new generation, advance dialogue and debate in Christian ethics, and inspire more faithful discipleship just as it honors one whom the contributors consider a mentor.   *978-1-57312-695-3 234 pages/pb* **$18.00**

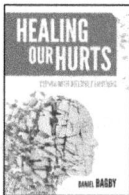

Healing Our Hurts
Coping with Difficult Emotions
Daniel Bagby

In *Healing Our Hurts*, Daniel Bagby identifies and explains all the dynamics at play in these complex emotions. Offering practical biblical insights to these feelings, he interprets faith-based responses to separate overly religious piety from true, natural human emotion. This book helps us learn how to deal with life's difficult emotions in a redemptive and responsible way. *978-1-57312-613-7 144 pages/pb* **$15.00**

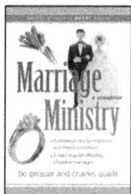

Marriage Ministry: A Guidebook
Bo Prosser and Charles Qualls

This book is equally helpful for ministers, for nearly/newlywed couples, and for thousands of couples across our land looking for fresh air in their marriages. *1-57312-432-X 160 pages/pb* **$16.00**

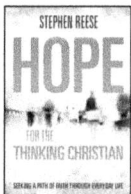

Hope for the Thinking Christian
Seeking a Path of Faith through Everyday Life
Stephen Reese

Readers who want to confront their faith more directly, to think it through and be open to God in an individual, authentic, spiritual encounter will find a resonant voice in Stephen Reese.
978-1-57312-553-6 160 pages/pb **$16.00**

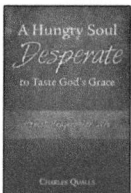

A Hungry Soul Desperate to Taste God's Grace
Honest Prayers for Life
Charles Qualls

Part of how we *see* God is determined by how we *listen* to God. There is so much noise and movement in the world that competes with images of God. This noise would drown out God's beckoning voice and distract us. Charles Qualls's newest book offers readers prayers for that journey toward the meaning and mystery of God. *978-1-57312-648-9 152 pages/pb* **$14.00**

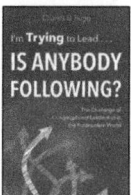

I'm Trying to Lead... Is Anybody Following?
The Challenge of Congregational Leadership in the Postmodern World
Charles B. Bugg

Bugg provides us with a view of leadership that has theological integrity, honors the diversity of church members, and reinforces the brave hearts of church leaders who offer vision and take risks in the service of Christ and the church. *978-1-57312-731-8 136 pages/pb* **$13.00**

James M. Dunn and Soul Freedom

Aaron Douglas Weaver

James Milton Dunn, over the last fifty years, has been the most aggressive Baptist proponent for religious liberty in the United States. Soul freedom—voluntary, uncoerced faith and an unfettered individual conscience before God—is the basis of his understanding of church-state separation and the historic Baptist basis of religious liberty.   *978-1-57312-590-1 224 pages/pb* **$18.00**

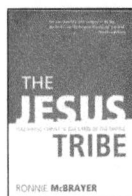

The Jesus Tribe
Following Christ in the Land of the Empire

Ronnie McBrayer

The Jesus Tribe fleshes out the implications, possibilities, contradictions, and complexities of what it means to live within the Jesus Tribe and in the shadow of the American Empire.

978-1-57312-592-5 208 pages/pb **$17.00**

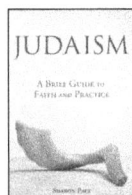

Judaism
A Brief Guide to Faith and Practice

Sharon Pace

Sharon Pace's newest book is a sensitive and comprehensive introduction to Judaism. What is it like to be born into the Jewish community? How does belief in the One God and a universal morality shape the way in which Jews see the world? How does one find meaning in life and the courage to endure suffering? How does one mark joy and forge community ties?   *978-1-57312-644-1 144 pages/pb* **$16.00**

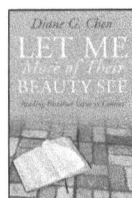

Let Me More of Their Beauty See
Reading Familiar Verses in Context

Diane G. Chen

Let Me More of Their Beauty See offers eight examples of how attention to the historical and literary settings can safeguard against taking a text out of context, bring out its transforming power in greater dimension, and help us apply Scripture appropriately in our daily lives.

978-1-57312-564-2 160 pages/pb **$17.00**

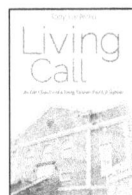

Living Call
An Old Church and a Young Minister Find Life Together

Tony Lankford

This light look at church and ministry highlights the dire need for fidelity to the vocation of church leadership. It also illustrates Lankford's conviction that the historic, local congregation has a beautiful, vibrant, and hopeful future.   *978-1-57312-702-8 112 pages/pb* **$12.00**

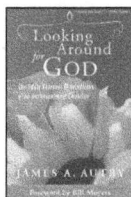

Looking Around for God
The Strangely Reverent Observations of an Unconventional Christian
James A. Autry

Looking Around for God, Autry's tenth book, is in many ways his most personal. In it he considers his unique life of faith and belief in God. Autry is a former Fortune 500 executive, author, poet, and consultant whose work has had a significant influence on leadership thinking.

978-157312-484-3 *144 pages/pb* **$16.00**

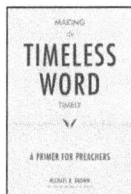

Making the Timeless Word Timely
A Primer for Preachers
Michael B. Brown

Michael Brown writes, "There is a simple formula for sermon preparation that creates messages that apply and engage whether your parish is rural or urban, young or old, rich or poor, five thousand members or fifty." The other part of the task, of course, involves being creative and insightful enough to know how to take the general formula for sermon preparation and make it particular in its impact on a specific congregation. Brown guides the reader through the formula and the skills to employ it with excellence and integrity.

978-1-57312-578-9 *160 pages/pb* **$16.00**

Meeting Jesus Today
For the Cautious, the Curious, and the Committed
Jeanie Miley

Meeting Jesus Today, ideal for both individual study and small groups, is intended to be used as a workbook. It is designed to move readers from studying the Scriptures and ideas within the chapters to recording their journey with the Living Christ.

978-1-57312-677-9 *320 pages/pb* **$19.00**

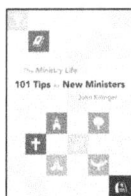

The Ministry Life
101 Tips for New Ministers
John Killinger

Sharing years of wisdom from more than fifty years in ministry and teaching, *The Ministry Life: 101 Tips for New Ministers* by John Killinger is filled with practical advice and wisdom for a minister's day-to-day tasks as well as advice on intellectual and spiritual habits to keep ministers of any age healthy and fulfilled.

978-1-57312-662-5 *244 pages/pb* **$19.00**

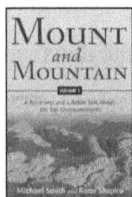

Mount and Mountain
Vol. 1: A Reverend and a Rabbi Talk About the Ten Commandments
Rami Shapiro and Michael Smith

Mount and Mountain represents the first half of an interfaith dialogue—a dialogue that neither preaches nor placates but challenges its participants to work both singly and together in the task of reinterpreting sacred texts. Mike and Rami discuss the nature of divinity, the power of faith, the beauty of myth and story, the necessity of doubt, the achievements, failings, and future of religion, and, above all, the struggle to live ethically and in harmony with the way of God.   *978-1-57312-612-0 144 pages/pb* **$15.00**

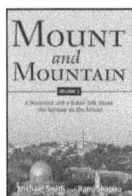

Mount and Mountain
Vol. 2: A Reverend and a Rabbi Talk About the Sermon on the Mount
Rami Shapiro and Michael Smith

This book, focused on the Sermon on the Mount, represents the second half of Mike and Rami's dialogue. In it, Mike and Rami explore the text of Jesus' sermon cooperatively, contributing perspectives drawn from their lives and religious traditions and seeking moments of illumination.   *978-1-57312-654-0 254 pages/pb* **$19.00**

Of Mice and Ministers
Musings and Conversations About Life, Death, Grace, and Everything
Bert Montgomery

With stories about pains, joys, and everyday life, *Of Mice and Ministers* finds Jesus in some unlikely places and challenges us to do the same. From tattooed women ministers to saying the "N"-word to the brotherly kiss, Bert Montgomery takes seriously the lesson from Psalm 139—where can one go that God is not already there?   *978-1-57312-733-2 154 pages/pb* **$14.00**

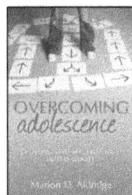

Overcoming Adolescence
Growing Beyond Childhood into Maturity
Marion D. Aldridge

In *Overcoming Adolescence*, Marion D. Aldridge poses questions for adults of all ages to consider. His challenge to readers is one he has personally worked to confront: to grow up *all the way*—mentally, physically, academically, socially, emotionally, and spiritually. The key involves not only knowing how to work through the process but also how to recognize what may be contributing to our perpetual adolescence.

978-1-57312-577-2 156 pages/pb **$17.00**

To order call **1-800-747-3016** or visit **www.helwys.com**

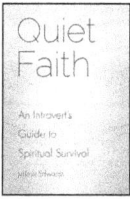

Quiet Faith
An Introvert's Guide to Spiritual Survival
Judson Edwards

In eight finely crafted chapters, Edwards looks at key issues like evangelism, interpreting the Bible, dealing with doubt, and surviving the church from the perspective of a confirmed, but sometimes reluctant, introvert. In the process, he offers some provocative insights that introverts will find helpful and reassuring. *978-1-57312-681-6 144 pages/pb* **$15.00**

Reading Ezekiel (Reading the Old Testament series)
A Literary and Theological Commentary
Marvin A. Sweeney

The book of Ezekiel points to the return of YHWH to the holy temple at the center of a reconstituted Israel and creation at large. As such, the book of Ezekiel portrays the purging of Jerusalem, the Temple, and the people, to reconstitute them as part of a new creation at the conclusion of the book. With Jerusalem, the Temple, and the people so purged, YHWH stands once again in the holy center of the created world.

978-1-57312-658-8 264 pages/pb **$22.00**

Reading Hosea–Micah
(Reading the Old Testament series)
A Literary and Theological Commentary
Terence E. Fretheim

Terence E. Fretheim explores themes of indictment, judgment, and salvation in Hosea–Micah. The indictment against the people of God especially involves issues of idolatry, as well as abuse of the poor and needy. The effects of such behaviors are often horrendous in their severity. While God is often the subject of such judgments, the consequences, like fruit, grow out of the deed itself. *978-1-57312-687-8 224 pages/pb* **$22.00**

Sessions with Genesis (Session Bible Studies series)
The Story Begins
Tony W. Cartledge

Immersing us in the book of Genesis, Tony W. Cartledge examines both its major stories and the smaller cycles of hope and failure, of promise and judgment. Genesis introduces these themes of divine faithfulness and human failure in unmistakable terms, tracing Israel's beginning to the creation of the world and professing a belief that Israel's particular history had universal significance. *978-1-57312-636-6 144 pages/pb* **$14.00**

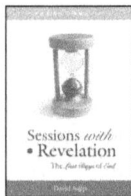

Sessions with Revelation (Session Bible Studies series)
The Final Days of Evil
David Sapp

David Sapp's careful guide through Revelation demonstrates that it is a letter of hope for believers; it is less about the last days of history than it is about the last days of evil. Without eliminating its mystery, Sapp unlocks Revelation's central truths so that its relevance becomes clear. *978-1-57312-706-6 166 pages/pb* **$14.00**

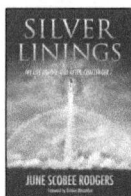

Silver Linings
My Life Before and After *Challenger 7*
June Scobee Rodgers

We know the public story of *Challenger 7*'s tragic destruction. That day, June's life took a new direction that ultimately led to the creation of the Challenger Center and to new life and new love. Her story of Christian faith and triumph over adversity will inspire readers of every age. *978 1-57312-570-3 352 pages/hc* **$28.00**

978-1-57312-694-6 352 pages/pb **$18.00**

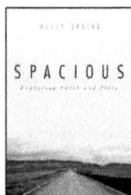

Spacious
Exploring Faith and Place
Holly Sprink

Exploring where we are and why that matters to God is an ongoing process. If we are present and attentive, God creatively and continuously widens our view of the world. *978-1-57312-649-6 156 pages/pb* **$16.00**

The Teaching Church
Congregation as Mentor
Christopher M. Hamlin / Sarah Jackson Shelton

Collected in *The Teaching Church: Congregation as Mentor* are the stories of the pastors who shared how congregations have shaped, nurtured, and, sometimes, broken their resolve to be faithful servants of God. *978-1-57312-682-3 112 pages/pb* **$13.00**

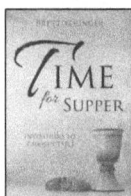

Time for Supper
Invitations to Christ's Table
Brett Younger

Some scholars suggest that every meal in literature is a communion scene. Could every meal in the Bible be a communion text? Could every passage be an invitation to God's grace? At the Lord's Table we experience sorrow, hope, friendship, and forgiveness. These meditations on the Lord's Supper help us listen to the myriad of ways God invites us to gratefully, reverently, and joyfully share the cup of Christ. *978-1-57312-720-2 246 pages/pb* **$18.00**

To order call **1-800-747-3016** or visit **www.helwys.com**

A Time to Laugh
Humor in the Bible
Mark E. Biddle

An extension of his well-loved seminary course on humor in the Bible, *A Time to Laugh* draws on Mark E. Biddle's command of Hebrew language and cultural subtleties to explore the ways humor was intentionally incorporated into Scripture. With characteristic liveliness, Biddle guides the reader through the stories of six biblical characters who did rather unexpected things.

978-1-57312-683-0 164 pages/pb **$14.00**

The World Is Waiting for You
Celebrating the 50th Ordination Anniversary of Addie Davis
Pamela R. Durso & LeAnn Gunter Johns, eds.

Hope for the church and the world is alive and well in the words of these gifted women. Keen insight, delightful observations, profound courage, and a gift for communicating the good news are woven throughout these sermons. The Spirit so evident in Addie's calling clearly continues in her legacy.

978-1-57312-732-5 224 pages/pb **$18.00**

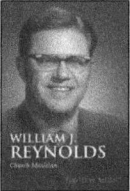

William J. Reynolds
Church Musician
David W. Music

William J. Reynolds is renowned among Baptist musicians, music ministers, song leaders, and hymnody students. In eminently readable style, David W. Music's comprehensive biography describes Reynolds's family and educational background, his career as a minister of music, denominational leader, and seminary professor.

978-1-57312-690-8 358 pages/pb **$23.00**

With Us in the Wilderness
Finding God's Story in Our Lives
Laura A. Barclay

What stories compose your spiritual biography? In *With Us in the Wilderness*, Laura Barclay shares her own stories of the intersection of the divine and the everyday, guiding readers toward identifying and embracing God's presence in their own narratives.

978-1-57312-721-9 120 pages/pb **$13.00**

To order call **1-800-747-3016** or visit **www.helwys.com**